Marion H Wood
3574 N.E Alameda
Por

D0392614

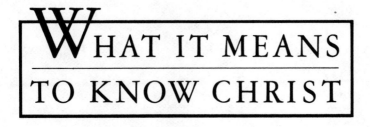

WHAT IT MEANS
TO KNOW CHRIST

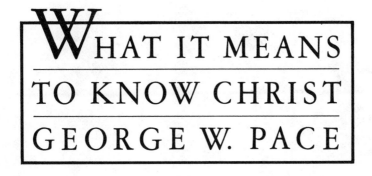

WHAT IT MEANS
TO KNOW CHRIST
GEORGE W. PACE

Council Press
Provo, Utah

ABOUT GEORGE PACE

George W. Pace was born on October 10, 1929, the youngest of 12 children. The son of Presley (Pres) Pace (Sheriff of Burley, Idaho, for 18 years) and Agnes Judd, he was raised on a farm in Burley. While attending Burley High, he was active in athletics and in school politics. Prior to his mission in 1950-52 to the Western Canadian Mission, he attended Utah State University. After his mission he attended BYU, where he met the former Miss Oregon, Diane Carman, of Portland, Oregon. They were married on December 17, 1954, in the Salt Lake Temple. Brother and Sister Pace are presently the parents of 12 children (ten daughters and two sons). They lived in Burley for the first five years of their marriage where Brother Pace farmed and taught seminary.

After completing his bachelors degree in political science at BYU, the Paces moved to Fort Collins, Colorado. While in Fort Collins, he opened and directed the LDS Institute of Religion at Colorado State University, where he obtained his master's degree in counseling. They then moved to California where he directed the LDS Institute of Religion at Stanford University. He received his doctorate at BYU in 1976 in religious education.

Brother Pace has taught as an associate professor at the "Y" since 1967, and has been on several LDS Church writing committees. He was selected by the student body to be "Professor of the Year" at Brigham Young University for 1978.

Brother Pace has served as a branch president at the Mission Training Center in Provo, on several high councils, and as a counselor in a stake presidency. On April 16, 1978, he was called to be the stake president of the BYU 10th Stake. He is a popular lecturer in the BYU Education Week and "Know Your Religion" series, and has led numerous tours to Israel.

In addition to this volume, Brother Pace has arranged and compiled the book, "The Faith of Young Mormons" and has written several articles for the LDS Church magazines. He is also featured in a series of taped lectures.

INTRODUCTION

After all the books that have been written about the Savior and various gospel principles, here is a book that strikes at the very heart of the gospel of Jesus Christ.

Don't make the mistake of assuming that this is a dry, philosophical discussion of religious abstractions. It isn't, not by any definition. It is a warm, personal and entertaining account of one man's humble struggle to know the Savior, a struggle that continued over many years, through many experiences—ranging from debates with sectarian theologians in front of large audiences, to solitary hikes to the tops of lonely mountains to plead hour after hour for a surer knowledge and a stronger faith in the Savior of this world.

This book is the expanded testimony of a master story teller, and one of the greatest teachers in the Church. It is the story of a modern-day Enos and his wrestle to know his Lord. The friendly, entertaining, and sincere style of George Pace draws the reader into the story in a way that the reader wants to do it too, develop that same relationship.

What It Means To Know Christ is a how-to book dealing with the most important relationship in life, the one between you and your Lord.

Every Latter-day Saint, who is serious about his or her religion, will find within these pages a quiet re-awakening of spiritual yearnings, a desire to sweep away the chaff of life and get to the very heart of things, to develop a real and personal relationship with Christ. Every sincere Latter-day Saint should read this book.

CONTENTS

FOREWORD

Over the years I have been stimulated by the scriptures and the writings of the General Authorities to do all in my power to know the Savior and develop a personal relationship with Him.

In my years as a teacher, it's been my intent to help students likewise develop their own personal relationship with the Savior. And I find that much of my students' greatest encouragement comes from my sharing experiences of a highly personal nature.

Thus, in preparing this book I have deliberately tried to retain the personal dimension of my own experiences. I don't wish to attract undue attention to myself. But rather I hope that my own experiences will help other people to center their lives in Christ and to develop their own personal relationship with Him. That is my central purpose.

I'm grateful to my wife Diane for her encouragement, her helpful criticisms and suggestions. It is to her and my precious children that I dedicate this work.

I am grateful to Carolyn McClusky, a former secretary, for her encouragement and to Kathy Grant who spent many, many hours editing and typing the manuscript.

I have tried to harmonize the ideas presented in this book with the scriptures and the position of the Church. But I assume full responsibility for what I have written.

I hope that what is contained herein will be helpful in some way to encourage people to realize that the point and purpose of the gospel is to introduce the Savior fully to the inhabitants of the Earth.

George W. Pace

Chapter 1

The Pearl Of
Greatest Price

In the church and kingdom of God, there are many "pearls of
great price," but one pearl is of greatest price, of greatest value—
what is it? Is it a testimony of Christ, of Joseph Smith, of the overall
divinity of the great latter-day work? Is it personal revelation or
freedom from sin, ignorance, and death?

There is no question that these are each pearls, but as I have
reflected on the simple two-sentence parable from which we have
taken the name of our fourth standard work, it seems to me that the
pearl of *greatest* price is a dynamic personal relationship with
Christ!

Acknowledging that Jesus is the Savior and Redeemer of the
world, my central theme in the chapters that follow is the tremendous importance of coming to know Jesus Christ. It involves not
simply sensing the remarkable power that is available through the

gospel of Jesus Christ, but recognizing that he, Christ, is the very source of that power; it involves not merely having a testimony of the divinity of the restored Church, but actually acquiring through that restored Church a profound knowledge of, commitment to, and personal friendship with the very Creator of heaven and earth. What I would like to explore with you has to do with placing the many pearls of the gospel, as it were, in perspective so as to accentuate that pearl of greatest price, recognizing that the full value of those pearls is seen when you and I accept them and use them as a means of developing a full and complete relationship with the Savior.

Even to approach the topic of what it means to know Christ is an awesome undertaking and one that would be out of the question if I didn't know that Jesus is the Christ, the literal and eternal Son of God. I know that through faith in Christ we can be forgiven of our sins, have our fallen nature changed, and enjoy an abhorrence for sin. I know that Jehovah is a God of power, for I have seen him make bare his mighty arm and enable the otherwise impossible to be accomplished. I know that the Lord is a God of love who can bestow upon us his infinite love to where we think our very flesh will be consumed (2 Nephi 4:21). The promise has been burned into my soul by the whisperings of the Spirit that if we are faithful in keeping the commandments and honoring every word that proceeds forth from the mouth of God, we will come to know the Savior marvelously well; and in time, the Lord will transform us in his image and ultimately we may have the privilege, perhaps while yet in mortality, of seeing his face.

The capstone of my testimony and the thrust of what I have to say is that we can come to know the Savior better than we know any other person on earth—that the Savior can have, and indeed must have, a greater impact on our lives than the combined impact of everyone else we know!

From Belief to Faith

My own experience of gradually growing in an awareness of the Savior himself and his place as the center of all things I'm sure is not atypical. I was raised as an active member of a small country ward in southern Idaho. I sensed early in my life that the testimonies I heard in the small frame chapel each fast and testimony meeting were sincere and indeed true. I felt very positive about the teachings I heard and the concepts I learned in the many auxiliary meetings I attended. I observed also that the more diligently I tried to keep the basic commandments and stay in close contact with the Church, although I often fell far short, the more peace I felt in my heart. And even though much of the motivation behind my activity in the Church was probably social (there were some really attractive girls in the ward), my overall involvement in the Church was uplifting and beneficial.

However, had I been asked in my late teens how I felt about the Church—that is, did I know the Church was true?—my response would have been something like, "I really think there is a strong possibility that the Church just might be true," or "There is absolutely no question in my mind that a lot of people I know really know the Church is true," or "Oh, I sure hope the Church is true!" In any event, even though I felt very good about the Church—indeed, there was absolutely no question in my mind that the overall impact of the Church in my life was quite positive—I knew there had to be much, much more to my membership. Somehow I sensed that I hadn't yet found that "pearl" which would give greater meaning to my membership in the Church and enable me to obtain a greater power to enjoy life more abundantly.

Somewhere along the line, I came to the conclusion that I desperately needed to learn more fully for myself by personal revelation that Joseph Smith was a prophet of God and that the true church of Jesus Christ indeed was restored to the earth. I determined that the quickest, surest way to do it was by reading the Book of Mormon and praying mightily about it. Consequently, in my nineteenth year and while farming my father's farm, I decided to tuck a copy of the Book of Mormon in my back pocket and take it with me everywhere I went. I carried out my plan, and whenever I got a chance between changes of water while irrigating, while waiting for the final preparation of my meals, and during every other spare moment I could find, I read the Book of Mormon with genuine intensity for the first time. I had, of course, read portions of it before, both in the auxiliaries and in seminary, but not really of my own volition and not with real intent. Along with diligently reading the Book of Mormon every time I got a chance, for the first time in my life I also lifted up my voice many times each day in mighty vocal prayer and pled for the witness of the Spirit.

My experience that summer of reading the Book of Mormon and fervently pouring out my heart in prayer changed my life more than any experience I had ever had. Before the summer was half over, it seemed I had walked into a whole new dimension of life. The unseen things of the Spirit started to become more real than the things of the world. There gradually deepened into my heart the unquestionable assurance that what I was reading was true, and with that revealed assurance, Joseph Smith's divine calling as a prophet of God emerged as the great anchor to the reality of the restoration of the gospel. With those assurances there seemed to come a desire to be more personally involved in the great unfolding drama of the redemption of man, a feeling that there was a preparation to be made, a mission to be fulfilled, a reason for being. Incidentally, I've noticed over the years that when anyone obtains a sure testimony of the divinity of the Church, invariably they will get excited about doing all they can to effectively build the kingdom. However, as beautiful and great as were those feelings, I still hadn't glimpsed what the real "pearl" was.

One experience I had that summer made a particularly deep impression on me and seemed to bring me a step closer to finding the pearl of greatest price. I had been irrigating alfalfa, a task that gave me several hours for reading and vocal prayer. About mid-morning, I was sitting on a railroad tie bridge that spanned the irrigation ditch, dangling my rubber boots in the water to keep them cool. As I sat there reading and reflecting, there came to me a quiet but particularly powerful witness of the Spirit that what I was reading was true. The feeling was so intense that I instinctively glanced heavenward. Although I didn't see anyone or hear anything, I seemed to feel strongly the presence of Nephi—so strongly, in fact, that I wouldn't have been at all surprised to see him standing there. It seemed to me that he spoke to my heart, and said: "George, I want you to know that what you're reading is true, for I wrote it. I want you to know that I have seen the Lord and talked with him. I have been carried by the wings of his Spirit to the tops of high mountains and have been shown marvelous things. And I want you to know he has given me great power to fulfill all the commandments he has given me."

What a great assurance it was for me to feel so deeply and powerfully the truth of Nephi's words, and especially to know of his relationship with the Lord and of the great power the Lord had given him. However, as the summer continued and I persisted in reading and lifting up my voice in prayer, there came into my heart by the power of the Spirit an even greater and more exciting idea; an idea that brought me a giant step closer to what it's really all about. Again, it seemed to come personally from Nephi, and he seemed to say to my heart: "It's wonderful that you now know that what I have written is true, and that you know I have seen and talked with Christ and have received of his marvelous power in my life. But it is *even more important for you to know that you, too, can see him as I have seen him; that you, too, can talk with him as I have; and that you, too, can obtain his mighty power to help you accomplish all he would have you do.*"

What an electrifying, soul-transforming thought that was to me!

It has continued to be the mainspring of my spiritual motivation and the greatest idea planted in my heart through the restored gospel.

I was to discover later that the prophet Joseph had taught this very principle, which confirmed in my heart the idea that Nephi had seemed to relate to me. Joseph said:

> God hath not revealed anything to Joseph, but what He will make known unto the Twelve, and even the least Saint may know all things as fast as he is able to bear them. (*Teachings of the Prophet Joseph Smith*, p. 324.)

He stated further that:

> Reading the experience of others, or the revelations given to *them* can never give *us* a comprehensive view of our condition and true relation to God. Knowledge of these things can only be obtained by experience through the ordinances of God set forth for that purpose. (Ibib., p. 324.)

I began to see the connection between Nephi's knowledge of and relationship to the Savior and the power of revelation he enjoyed. I began to realize that his ability to explain Isaiah so beautifully, to teach the doctrine of Christ so powerfully, to work such a mighty and everlasting work, came because he knew the Savior so well. But even more important was the realization that he was saying, in effect, "You can know him, even Christ, as well as I do and in knowing him you will enjoy his marvelous power even as I have done."

What a great appreciation I feel for Nephi and for all the prophets for having inspired me with those great ideas, for they have changed my life. Surely all of us are grateful for the tremendous testimonies of others that Jesus is the Christ, that he is a God of power, a God of miracles. But unless each of us experiences the reality of the Savior, comes to know him as they have, and comes to enjoy the self-same power, we have failed to take advantage of their testimonies and we have failed to receive the greatest blessing the church and kingdom of God can bestow upon us.

The gradual awakenings in my heart that it is possible to know the Lord and to know him well—and that not only is it possible, but absolutely necessary for eternal life (John 17:3)—began to kindle within me a greater and greater desire to learn of him. I determined to use the Spirit more effectively, to try more diligently to magnify my callings in the priesthood and to try to understand how all the programs and efforts of the church and kingdom of God could bring me to the marvelous relationship I desperately desired. As the years slipped by, special experiences I had from time to time seemed to beckon me to strive more diligently to know fully the Lord—experiences that reminded me powerfully that if I would center my life in Christ, if I would see him as the source of all blessings, if I would "root" the ordinances, principles, and the priesthood in him, the divine Redeemer, if everything I was to do would be done to bring him honor and glory, then in time I would know him better than I knew anyone else on earth.

One of the experiences that kept alive my hope that someday I could know the Savior as well as the prophets do occurred while I was in the mission home in Salt Lake City just prior to leaving on my mission. The particular setting was old Barrett Hall on Temple Square (the hall has since been torn down). There were approximately three hundred missionaries assembled to be instructed by different brethren, most of whom were General Authorities. I remember Don Colton, the mission home president, announcing the next speaker, whose topic was the atonement of Christ. I had not heard of this particular man and had no idea what to expect, but as his talk on the atonement unfolded, I felt the fire of the Spirit come into my heart with a greater intensity than I had ever felt before. I knew without question that the man speaking enjoyed a deep and profound relationship with the Savior—an understanding and relationship that went far beyond the words he used. I felt a strong assurance that some day I too could know the Lord as well as the good man who was speaking. I say assurance, but in that most profound feeling that came I felt an invitation—a powerful invitation—to come to know the Lord, and with that assurance and invitation I vowed with all the energy of my heart that some day I would! It is significant that of all the beautiful, meaningful talks I heard in the mission home, no other left such a lasting, motivating impression on my heart as did this one. I am sure I will forever hold in high esteem the first mortal who successfully fired my entire being with the idea that I too could know Christ.

Several years later, in my first year of married life, I enjoyed another experience of a very similar nature. It was a windy spring day, a Saturday, and the weekend of General Conference. Even though I was preparing a field for planting and had a lot of harrowing to do, I stopped the tractor, jumped off, and hurried over to the little house we were living in to listen to the morning session. As I opened the kitchen door, I was greeted with the voice of President J. Reuben Clark and the sight of my wife standing in the tiny front room ironing. Not wanting to miss any of the words that President Clark was speaking, my wife and I nodded at each other and I walked through the kitchen, squeezed past her and the ironing board, and sat down. President Clark was speaking about the Savior, bearing an eloquent and powerful testimony of him and his divine mission, when again the Spirit came like fire into my heart. His words were not unusual, but the power with which he spoke to my heart was extraordinary. The assurance came that this great man knew the Savior, and again the invitation came by the Spirit that I could know the Lord as well, and I vowed that some day I would.

On another occasion years later, the circumstances were different but the experience was similar, only of greater intensity. Just that day, the opening day of conference, I had returned from a 50 mile hike with thirty boy scouts. I had gathered the family together in the family room to watch the conference proceedings. President Harold B. Lee announced the next speaker and as he did, I remember being unusually excited about the opportunity of hearing that individual talk. As the speaker commenced, he indicated he wanted to talk about the Savior. Up to that time in my life I had never been so deeply touched by a testimony of Christ as I was that day. The Spirit was so intense, so powerful, that I could hardly hear with my outer ears. I felt a desire to know the Savior with a perfect knowledge that was more intense than I had ever felt. I believe I shall never forget in time or eternity the impact of that classic talk.

It is important to remember that every principle of the gospel and every commandment is significant and plays such a vital role in our salvation and exaltation. We desperately need to know the entire gospel, to catch a vision of the width and depth of the entire plan of salvation, to know the mysteries as well as the practical day by day things; but I would be remiss as a member of the Church if I did not declare with every fiber of my being that that which has changed my life the most, that which has caused me to want to serve others the most, is the idea that I can know the Savior myself. It isn't enough to know his gospel, his commandments, the doctrine of the priesthood; we must, in addition, know the Master.

In the following pages, I want to elaborate on the idea that all things—all creation and all of Heavenly Father's dealings with men on earth—point to and center in Christ. Once this idea is embedded in our hearts, the marvelous impact of a Savior-centered universe will reveal the reality and majesty of the Savior in such a way that with every breath and thought we will acknowledge him, and our every action will be to his honor and glory.

All Things Point to Christ

I attended a Sunday School lesson on Abraham's sacrifice of Isaac. I was somewhat intrigued that the lesson was presented, discussed, and summarized without any mention of the Savior's atoning sacrifice. The principles of faith and obedience were quite effectively explored, but I couldn't help but feel that the greater message of imagery or typology foreshadowing the sacrifice of the Lord was completely missed. I was disappointed because I had been convinced from my scripture study that, as Nephi stated, "All things which have been given of God from the beginning of the world, unto man, are the typifying of him." (2 Nephi 11:4.), and felt this surely was specifically the case with Abraham's experience.

What a thought it is to realize that everything given from God to man is given that it might typify Christ and direct our attention fully to him, that we might comprehend his atonement and his gospel. The very heavens and the earth are created to bear record of him (Moses 6:63). Christ is the light of the sun, the moon, and the stars (D&C 88:7-9). He it is who lights every man who comes into the world (John 1:9), and it is he who enables us to live, move, and have our being (Acts 17:28). To see the sun in its majesty, the heavenly planets moving in their courses, the light reflecting from the eyes of others, to enjoy life in its infinitely varied forms, indeed, to experience spiritual life moment by moment is to see the Savior in and through all things.

In addition, the experiences and events of the scriptures are also in similitude of Christ. One is well within the mark to state that these experiences and events are veritable gold mines of revelation about the Savior. Consider the powerful message in the experience of Moses offering deliverance to the Israelites who were dying from the bites of the poisonous serpents. Moses lifted a brazen serpent high on a pole and promised that all who would look would live. This was done in similitude of the Savior being lifted on the cross that "as many as should look upon the Son of God with faith, having a contrite spirit, might live, even unto that life which is eternal." (Helaman 8:15.) The Liahona given to Lehi's colony to guide them to the promised land would only work on the basis of faith in Christ. Each of us as members of the Church have our own personal Liahona in the gift of the Holy Ghost. If we will give heed, the Holy Ghost will teach us the words of Christ and guide us through this vale of sorrow into a far better land of promise (Alma 37:43-46).

To look in more detail at how all things indeed point to Christ, let's review closely the one experience that is seen as the classic test that man has endured to show his faith, obedience and love to God, but which is more especially in similitude of the sacrifice of Christ (Jacob 4:5). That experience is Abraham's call to offer his son, Isaac, as a human sacrifice.

Abraham, even though his father turned away from righteousness and in spite of living in an idolatrous society, became a mighty man of faith. Without question, he had been taught the sanctity of life and loathed the practice of human sacrifice which was so prevalent in his day. In fact, Abraham had once been a victim at the sacrificial altar of the wicked priests of Elkenah and was delivered at the last moment through the miraculous intervention of an angel.

In time, Abraham was invited by the Lord to leave the land of his fathers, the Ur of the Chaldees, and travel to the land of Canaan. It was shortly after his arrival in this new land that Abraham became aware of his marvelous destiny. One night as the starry heavens shone forth in their resplendent glory, Jehovah appeared to Abraham, and in a face to face conversation, informed him that he would become the father of nations and that his seed would be more numerous than the stars in the sky and the sands on the seashore (Abraham 3:14). The Lord told Abraham that through him and the priesthood he bore, all nations of the earth would be blessed. Abraham had lived so close to the Lord, and now to have the privilege of seeing the face of the Lord, to hear with his own ears the voice of truth which would distill such unbelievable peace and comfort into the very center of his soul, and to know in such a perfect way that he and Sarah would be blessed with innumerable posterity—how these heaven-sent assurances must have thrilled his entire being.

Yet Abraham was close to 75 years old when Jehovah appeared to him in Canaan, and the years quickly slipped by without Sarah conceiving a child. When he was 86, Abraham had been blessed with a son, Ishmael, by Sarah's handmaiden, Hagar; however, when Ismael was thirteen, the Lord spoke to Abraham, stressing that the promised covenant was not to be fulfilled through Ishmael. At this point the Lord told Abraham, "But my covenant will I establish with Isaac which Sarah shall bear unto thee at this set time in the next year." (Genesis 17:21.)

It is particularly from this point on that there emerges a remarkable typology or foreshadowing of the life and mission of the Savior which increases in its dramatic nature as the lives of Abraham and Sarah, continue to unfold. Abraham was approaching his 100th birthday and Sarah was nearly 90 when they learned that Sarah would conceive and bring forth a son whose name would be Isaac. The similitude of Isaac's birth to that of the Savior's is initially seen in the incredulous reaction of both Sarah and Mary to the announcement that each would conceive. Angelic visitors offered to both the assurance of the Lord's power: In response to Sarah's disbelief, an angel said, "With God nothing shall be impossible" (I.V. Genesis 18:13), and Mary was asked, "Is anything too hard for the Lord?" (Luke 1:37.) The miraculous conception by one so old as Sarah was at the time is in similitude of the miraculous manner in which Mary conceived that she might give birth to the literal Son of God. Sarah would give birth to her only son as Mary would give birth to the Only Behotten Son of God. Isaac would come forth as a child of promise through whom all generations of the earth would be blessed. The Savior would come forth as *the* child of promise, through whom all people in all generations of time would be blessed. Isaac was a man of faith in similitude of the faith and righteousness of the Savior. Abraham delighted in his son and loved him dearly, even as the Father loved the Son (Matthew 3:17).

I personally cannot imagine more ideal circumstances than those of Abraham and Isaac in which God could test the faith and obedience of one of his children. Yet not only was Abraham to be proven a man of perfect faith, but in the process of manifesting that faith, he would come to know in a deep and personal way what it would cost the Father to send his Son as a human sacrifice for the sins of the world.

I'm sure there is no way the human tongue could describe the feelings that must have come into Abraham's heart when his God, even Jehovah, appeared to him and without any explanation, commanded Abraham to offer Isaac as a burnt offering (Genesis 22:2). Can one even imagine the struggle that was Abraham's as he realized that this command seemingly would nullify the promises God had made? After having lived a life of total obedience to God, how difficult it must have been for Abraham, in order to maintain that obedience, to follow the command to slay his precious son. For Abraham, who loved life, whose life had been preserved from the horrible death of a sacrificial victim, now even to contemplate thrusting a dagger into his own son's heart must have sent shudders into the depths of his soul. Yet in spite of his heart strings being pulled to the very breaking point, Abraham immediately prepared to fulfill the terrifying command by traveling with Isaac and some servants to the land of Moriah.

Sacred writ is silent on Isaac's age when this experience occurred. He is referred to as a "lad" (Genesis 22:12); however, the term lad refers in the scriptures to a boy of about 17 (Genesis 37:2), a married man (Genesis 43:8), and Enoch called himself a lad when he was at least 65! (Moses 6:25, 31.) Interestingly enough, evidence in apocryphal writings suggests that at the time this experience occurred, Isaac could have been the same age as the Savior was at the time of his death.

After arriving at the base of the small mount called Moriah, Abraham laid upon Isaac's shoulders the wood upon which Isaac would be placed, even as the Savior, approximately 2,000 years later, would take upon his shoulders the wood or cross upon which he would be nailed. Abraham and Isaac ascended a small mount even as the Savior would ascend the small hill Golgotha. From all indications Isaac, like the Son of God, was a willing sacrifice. According to the Book of Jasher, as Abraham and Isaac climbed up to the top of the mount and Abraham explained why they were there, Isaac responded, "I will do all that the Lord spoke to thee with joy and cheerfulness of heart. . . . Blessed is the Lord who has this day chosen me to be a burnt offering before him." (Book of Jasher 23:52, 56.)

As the last embrace was shared, the final parting words spoken, and the knife lifted to the zenith of Abraham's reach, how Abraham must have understood the love God would manifest for him and for all mankind in sending his Son as a sacrifice for the sins of the world. Surely Abraham comprehended the meaning of Gethsemane and Golgotha like few mortals who have ever lived, and in that comprehension obtained a faith that earned for him celestial powers while yet in mortality and the fulfillment of all the promises Jehovah made to him. Thus, Abraham's experience with Isaac, like all great foreshadowings or typologies in the scriptures, has as its purpose pointing the way to Christ and his atoning sacrifice.

The Purpose of the Church

Simply put, the purpose of the restored Church as the sole repository of the fulness of the gospel of Jesus Christ on earth (D&C 1:30) is to teach the correct principles and administer the true ordinances that the power of godliness might flow into our lives. The Church, it seems to me, can fulfill its sacred trust and responsibility only as it is successful in helping people realize that redemption is because of Christ, that it centers in Christ, and that it flows from Christ through the ordinances of the gospel as we grasp, comprehend, and exercise the principle of faith in Christ. I don't think it can be said too strongly that redemption is not in the principles, ordinances, or programs of the Church but rather in Christ. The ordinances and the principles and the programs of the

Chruch are channels by which that power can flow into our lives if, again, we truly exercise faith in Christ.

The idea that the Savior is the source of the power of redemption, that we need desperately to know him and come to him, and that the Church and the gospel are the means to bring us to him is vividly portrayed in Lehi's dream of the tree of life. When Nephi sought for an interpretation of the tree of life or the love of God (1 Nephi 11:22), he was shown the birth, life, and mission (the atonement) of Christ. In other words, he came to understand that the tree of life, the central object of the dream, symbolizes Jesus Christ; walking along the path symbolizes embracing the Church and gospel of Christ; holding on to the iron rod symbolizes living by every word that proceeds from God through the scriptures, the living prophets and personal revelation, and partaking of the tree represents coming all the way to the Savior and partaking fully of the blessings and powers of his atonement—from all indications the greatest experience that can occur to man during his mortal probation.

It is impossible, according to this great vision, to come to Christ fully, to partake of his atonement, to have the promise of eternal life, unless we get on the path, unless we go through baptism of the water and Spirit, and move along the path clinging to the Iron Rod. However, we all need to be so careful as members of the Church to realize that getting on the path and moving along the path are two different things, and making it all the way to the tree and remaining faithful thereafter are two additionally distinct accomplishments. It appears that it is not an unusual experience for us as members of the Church to be so thrilled and excited about finding and being on the path (belonging to the true church) that we take up homestead on the path! How awful it would be to come to judgment day as members of the Church, having been on the path for years, and discover we had never made the journey all the way to the tree—all the way to Christ! Indeed, the path or membership in the divine Church is exciting, and the association with many wonderful people who share a common commitment is a great blessing in itself. The uplift and benefits from the Church programs are a great boon to all who will involve themselves in them. But if we think the path is great, wait till we make it to the tree! Then and only then will the central majesty of the Savior and his atonement be fully appreciated in our lives. Then and only then will the greater powers of heaven be ours to use in building the kingdom of God. Then and only then will the pure love of Christ be our personal gift and daily companion in the fullest sense. No wonder Lehi said the fruit of the tree of life was desirable above all other fruit (1 Nephi 8:12).

A simple analogy may be helpful. One summer evening a good friend of ours came to our home to take my wife and me to dinner. He drove up in a brand new Thunderbird, one of the most beautiful cars I had ever seen. It was white on white—everything was white. I imagined that if I were to open the hood, the engine would be white—the car probably even used white oil! As my friend pulled up alongside my 1961 Falcon, the contrast was almost more than I could bear. Even the tires on my Falcon suddenly seemed square in comparison!

The Thunderbird had a sun-roof, and I immediately asked if he would mind if I put a blanket on the front seat so I could stand with my body pushed up through the sun-roof. Then I suggested he drive all around town honking his horn so everyone who had seen me in my Falcon could now see me in such a fancy, beautiful car!

Often members of the Church use their membership in the Church as they would a beautiful, powerful car—the most beautiful, powerful car on earth. They drive the car all around, showing it off, honking quite loudly and telling everyone all about the car and how marvelous the car is and how absolutely necessary it is that everyone have a car exactly like it. Yet in all their frantic show-off efforts, they forget that a car has but one basic function—transportation. Likewise, our membership in the Church has essentially one great and grand purpose, and that is that we might successfully journey all the way to the Savior and that in achieving that goal we might be successful in bringing others to him.

My own experiences with members and new members of the Church have helped me realize that the challenge of using the gospel to come to Christ and of seeing the centrality of Christ in all things is a very real one, perhaps the greatest in the Church . We have too many people, both in and out of the Church who are exposed to the message of the restoration who see only the path and not the tree. Let me illustrate what I mean with a personal experience.

While serving as the director of the LDS Institute adjacent to Colorado State University in Fort Collins, Colorado, I was an active member of the University Religious Directors Association. At one of our monthly meetings, we were brainstorming for ideas that would stimulate more interest in religion on campus. As the discussion progressed, the idea evolved that one approach might be to offer free seminars on various Old and New Testament topics. I thought the idea was a good one and indicated that I would be happy to support the effort. The next idea that immediately surfaced was that the seminars must be non-denominational. I'm not sure why everyone looked at me when that idea came up, but quickly I said, "Naturally, they must be non-denominational." Most of the men looked a little incredulous when I volunteered to teach a course on the life and teachings of Paul. They mumbled something again about the importance of a very broad, non-denominational approach to any seminar taught. I sensed, in fact, that they felt the possibility of a Mormon institute director teaching a non-denominational seminar was highly unlikely, and I certainly couldn't argue with them on that point! However, my offer, among others, was accepted. A thorough advertisement campaign ensued, and on the appointed Friday, much to my delight, I found a room full of people who had signed up for my seminar.

Anyone who has spent much time reading Paul's life and his teachings is overwhelmed at the singularly powerful and Savior-centered testimony of that great apostle, who was one of the greatest missionaries of all time. His power was so great that irate

Jewish rulers referred to him as having "turned the whole world upside down." (Acts 17:6.) His message was direct and to the point: "I determine not to know anything among you save Jesus Christ and him crucified." (1 Corinthians 2:2.)

The course lasted five weeks and was an absolutely delightful teaching experience. I explained to the class that we wouldn't have time to explore the fascinating cultural peculiarities of the Greeks, Romans, or Jews, nor the geographical distances between the cities in which Paul preached. The emphasis was clearly on the doctrine of Christ.

Considering the potential for missionary work, I will admit it was quite hard not to wear my tailor-made vest that holds 50 copies of the pamphlet "Joseph Smith Tells His Own Story," and also very hard to deny the missionaries' request to hide behind the door. In fact, my commitment to the non-denominational idea was so strong that I even left my collapsible baptismal font at home!

As we discussed such "non-denominational" topics as divine authority, church organization, and baptism for the dead, I will admit that some questions became pretty difficult to handle. For example, as we discussed baptism, one class member raised his hand and inquired why I insisted on the idea that baptism was not for infants, but for those who were "as you would put it, Mr. Pace, accountable." I thought, "Oh how can I answer that question without having my angel Moroni pin suddenly appear to be ten feet tall!" Right at that moment, another class member abruptly spoke up and said, "I can tell you why Mr. Pace takes that position. Having studied a lot of psychology and sociology, I have become convinced that people aren't capable of really understanding what they are doing [aren't accountable] until somewhere between the ages of seven and nine!"

During the five week period the seminar was held, I had the opportunity to teach the doctrine of Christ with some depth. I told the students that I knew that through the ordinances of the gospel, Christ's divine nature could flow into our beings, and that if we would develop a meaningful relationship with the Savior, it would be possible, through the gifts of the Spirit, to have the image of Christ engraven upon our countenances.

The last session, I spent the entire hour simply bearing testimony that I knew that God lives and that Jesus is the Christ, the Son of God and the Savior and Redeemer of the world. In that concluding session I felt the Lord's Spirit there in a special way. After I bore my testimony, and I did it in the name of Jesus Christ, the entire group seemed subdued, yet very warm and responsive. Although I dismissed the class, no one immediately got up and left. They all just sat there with a special kind of reverence. Finally, someone raised his hand and gently asked, "Mr. Pace, would you mind telling us what church you belong to?"

I replied, "I would be very happy to tell you. I'm a member of the Church of Jesus Christ of Latter-day Saints, more commonly called the Mormon church."

As soon as I said that, there were audible gasps. I thought several students might even fall off of their chairs. One person in his amazement blurted out, "Mr. Pace, you're a Mormon and you've been teaching Jesus Christ to us the way you have?"

That comment hurt a great deal. It was disappointing to think that anyone would be surprised to learn that a Mormon would teach Jesus Christ in the way that I had. Into my mind came an unspoken response: "Young man, there is not anyone on the face of the earth who can teach Jesus Christ the way a Mormon can."

Incidentally, as the group began to leave, I hurriedly visited with as many members of the class as I could, asking if they, too, were surprised to learn that I was a Mormon. All those I spoke with responded that they *were* surprised. I then asked them if they personally were acquainted with any Latter-day Saints. It so happened that everyone I spoke with had lived next door to members of the Church.

As I walked home late that afternoon, I thought how unfortunate it was that any non-member could be exposed to any active Latter-day Saint and not know that the whole point and purpose of Joseph Smith and the restoration is to declare to a confused world that indeed Jesus Christ lives, that he has appeared and is appearing in our day, and that once again anyone who seeks with any kind of intensity can come to know him in a marvelous way.

Keeping our Eye on the Savior

Having visited the Holy Land on many different occasions, I've had the opportunity of crossing the Sea of Galilee quite a few times. Each time I do, numerous scriptural experiences in the life of the Savior come vividly to mind. One such experience which illustrates our need to center our lives in Christ is recorded in Matthew 12:26-32.

After the feeding of the five thousand, the Savior directed the Twelve to cross the Sea of Galilee and go to Capernaum; in due time he was to meet them in Bethsaida. But as they were crossing the sea, a great storm arose. They were making little progress toward their destination when, much to their amazement, they saw Jesus walking toward them across the waves. Initially the Twelve were frightened, but the Savior's speaking to them reassured them. Then, even though the Savior was coming to them, it seems that Peter just couldn't wait and he impetuously and boldly cried out, "Lord, if it be thou, bid me come unto thee on the water." Jesus replied, "Come."

The simple frankness of the invitation and Peter's excitement at seeing the Lord so kindled his faith that he climbed out of the boat and started walking on the water to his beloved Master. But when Peter "saw the wind boisterous, he was afraid; and beginning to sink, he cried, saying, Lord, save me."

I believe that Peter initially succeeded at walking on the water because he riveted his eye on the Savior, trusting implicitly in the Savior's admonition to "come" to him. Seemingly no other alternatives came into his mind. But I believe that as soon as Peter took his eyes off the Savior and admitted other considerations into his mind—the boisterous waves and the fact that he was doing something which seemed impossible—he immediately began to sink!

So it is with us. If we want our activity in the Church, our involvement with others, and the service we render to be consecrated to the welfare of our souls, we must keep our eyes riveted on the Savior. If we don't, we will be unable to keep ourselves on the right course—to enjoy a dynamic faith that can keep us from being swallowed up in the waves of humanism, of intellectual sophistry, and overwhelming materialism. Earth life is so ordained that there is no way we can successfully keep the commandments and accomplish all he would have us do unless it is by and through a daily Savior-centered faith.

I personally thrill in the Savior-centered witness of the prophets. I hear in their witnesses a challenge to each of us to come to know the Lord so well that in our living and teaching the gospel, in our serving and our administering the affairs of the kingdom, we will influence others to come into the kingdom of God and commit themselves wholeheartedly to know the Master, to come to him, and to be willing to build up his kingdom on the earth.

The prophet Joseph, in a letter to his wife Emma, stressed in a touching way his feeling about wanting to draw close to the Savior. The prophet, in company with Newell K. Whitney, had been away from home for some time and had not heard from his wife, but Brother Whitney had just received a letter. Joseph wrote:

> Sister Whitney wrote a letter to her husband which was very cheery. Being unwell at that time and filled with much anxiety, it would have been very consoling to me to have received a few lines from you. But ... I will try to be content with my lot knowing that God is my friend, in Him I shall find comfort. I have given my life into his hands. I am prepared to go at his call. *I desire to be with Christ. I count not my life dear to me only to do his will.* (Cited by LaMar C. Berrett in "An Impressive Letter From the Pen of Joseph Smith," *BYU Studies* 11 (Summer 1971):

Brigham Young expressed a beautiful invitation to know the Savior in the following words:

> The greatest and most important of all requirements of our Father in heaven and of his Son Jesus Christ is ... to believe in Jesus Christ, confess him, seek to know Him, cling to him, make friends with him. Take a course to open and keep open a communication with your Elder Brother or file-leader—our Savior. (*JD* 8:339.)

One of the most beautiful scriptural testimonies of Christ and most powerful invitations to come to know him is found in the following words of Moroni:

> And then at the judgment day shall ye know that I have seen Jesus, and that he hath talked with me face to face, and that he told me in plain humility, even as a man telleth another in mine own language, concerning these things. ... And now, I would commend you to seek this Jesus of whom the prophets and apostles have written, that the grace of God the Father, and also the Lord Jesus Christ, and the Holy Ghost, which beareth record of them, may be and abide in you forever. (Ether 12:39, 41.)

May we respond to Moroni's invitation to "seek this Jesus of whom the apostles and prophets have written." May we remember that message of Joseph Smith to all of us is that we, like him, can know the God of Abraham, Isaac and Jacob; that he, even Christ, can be heard, seen and felt. May we believe with all of our hearts that we can know him, for only in believing we can do so will our faith and consequent determination be great enough to achieve such a marvelous goal. And may the Lord bless each of us that we might be fully successful in finding, obtaining and keeping the pearl of greatest price!

Chapter 2

To Know The Lord
Is To Know We May Converse
With Him As One Man
Converses With Another

On one occasion I received an invitation to speak in sacrament meeting to some combined wards of BYU students the sabbath before Christmas. Because it was such a favorite time of the year, a time when a special spirit of brotherhood seems to pervade the earth, I felt especially desirous to speak in a meaningful way about the Savior and what it really means to know him.

For some time, the Lord's statement in John 17:3 had occupied my mind with unusual intensity. He declared, "For this is life eternal, that they might know thee the only true God, and Jesus Christ whom thou hast sent." I was convinced that when the Lord said we could know him, that is exactly what he meant—that we can take his words literally. I was also more and more intrigued with the idea that one's very eternal life is predicated on whether or not one knows the Father and the Son, recognizing that one comes to know the Son first, so that ultimately the Son might introduce him to the Father (Matthew 11:27, John 14:6).

I had gradually been obtaining stronger and stronger feelings about the Lord and felt I was becoming better acquainted with him. But as I began to prepare my talk, I felt I wanted to obtain some additional, specific ideas that would help myself and those to whom I was to speak come to a greater understanding of what it means to know him.

I remember approaching Heavenly Father in prayer. My question to him was simple and to the point: "How can I come to know more fully your Son?" Almost immediately a question came into my mind: "Of all the people you know on earth, whom do you know the best?" As I reflected for just a moment, the person who came directly to mind was my father. The thought came with considerable force, and it was also confirmed to me that I not only knew my father better than I knew any other person, but that I indeed knew him well!

Another question seemed to form in my mind: "What kind of experiences did you have with your earthly father that enabled you to know him so well?" I honestly wondered for a moment what all of this had to do with knowing Christ; and then all of a sudden the idea flooded into my mind that *the experiences I'd had in getting to know my dad were similar to the kinds of experiences I needed to have to really come to know the Savior!*

What a simple yet exciting idea that was to me! How marvelous it was to realize that experiences I was already well acquainted with through a great relationship with my father could be duplicated in my relationship with the Lord to help me come to know him in a powerful way. In fact, that particular idea did more to give me specific direction in seeking for a personal relationship with Christ than any previous idea I'd ever had.

Talking, Talking, Talking

On that occasion as I continued praying and thinking about my relationship with my father and the kinds of experiences I'd had with him that might assist me in developing a relationship with the Savior, many aspects of my relationship with Dad came into focus—such things as how deeply I admired him and wanted to become like him, how much it meant to me when he expressed openly his love and appreciation for me, how much it meant to have him embrace me warmly on occasion, the inestimable value of learning how to work by working with him. However, the very first idea that actually entered my mind was that I had spent a great deal of time talking with him. How the memories came—having lived on a farm, there had been hundreds of hours where we had many opportunities to talk. While milking cows, hauling hay, hoeing beets or irrigating, the chances were there and we took advantage of them. I could see clearly that a great deal of conversation with my father had been the primary means of enabling me to develop a tremendous relationship with him, and I realized that the very same principle was the key to developing a relationship with the Lord.

As I reflected further then and later, I found that many experiences in conversation with my father could give me practical direction in building my relationship with the Lord. Let me just elaborate with several specific examples.

I recalled that even as a very young boy, I had been elated to discover that any and all concerns and questions I had could be taken to my father. It was so easy to talk to him—he listened intently, showed interest, and always made me feel good. Because of this attitude on his part, I became willing to share with him more and more of my own feelings. By the time I was a teen-ager and confronted with some of the more serious decisions of my life, it was natural and easy for me to share my deepest concerns and anxieties with him and in turn receive significant counsel and direction.

It is the same with prayer. If we will be willing to share our problems, the small as well as the large, believing the Lord is interested in every and any concern, we will come to a point where we are willing and able to open our hearts to the Lord, to share the deepest feelings we have, and we will come to feel his marvelous comfort and direction in every phase of our lives.

Something that I know contributed greatly to my communication with my father and consequently my ability to know him so well was the desire and willingness on my part to go out of my way to talk to him. While farming on our hundred acres, I would frequently need to cross between different portions of the farm. Even though I was tremendously busy and often wondered if I should take the time, I would go out of my way considerably just to be able to pause for a few minutes to chat with him. And every time I put forth that extra effort, I came away grateful for every moment of time with him.

Another parallel to prayer can be drawn. It takes a lot of effort, a lot of going out of our way. But if we will be willing to sacrifice time and effort to find opportunities to pray mightily to him, we will come to learn that those times it takes everything we have to humble ourselves before the Lord are those times the veil becomes thinnest, and strength and comfort will be received above and beyond what we had imagined could be ours.

As the years slipped by and my conversations with Dad continued, I literally arrived at a point where I enjoyed talking to Dad more than I enjoyed talking with anyone else I knew. What a coveted goal to seek with the Lord! To love talking to him more than you love to talk to anyone else! I also could not remember a time when I looked forward to ending a conversation with my father—suggesting again a goal to achieve in prayer.

I came to appreciate even more completely the blessings of the meaningful communication my father and I had shared over the years through what was to be my last conversation with him.

At the time my family and I were living in Fort Collins, Colorado, where I directed the Institute of Religion at Colorado State University. I had traveled to Provo to attend a pre-school workshop for Institute directors, and afterwards I drove over to southern Idaho to visit my parents. My mother had died when I was nine, leaving eleven children, three of whom were then married. Dad had remarried, and the challenges of a second marriage continued to pose some concerns that prompted me to do all I could to help things go more smoothly.

After visiting with Dad and my stepmother, just before returning to Colorado, I walked with Dad out to the stockyards where we talked very seriously with each other for some time. Dad seemed a little discouraged, even a little unhappy. Out of a desire to give him a word of encouragement, I reminded him that in spite of life's ups and downs, it was all worth it. I told him that I hoped he would continue to be Christlike in all he said and did. Then, almost before I realized what I was saying, I boldly told him, "Dad, before you know it, this life will be over and you'll be back with Mother and all will be well." I'll not forget the look on his face as he responded, "Yes, yes, I know what you mean." Then he said, "George, let me share with you a beautiful experience I had with your mother many years after she passed away." He went on to relate in some detail a marvelous spiritual experience that had given him great comfort over the years. As he shared it with me I was, to say the least, grateful and comforted myself to know he had received such a strengthening experience.

We embraced, kissed each other, and I left. As I drove away, I felt without question that I had been especially honored to have Dad share with me such a sacred experience, and I knew he never would have done so had we not built a close relationship with each other by spending a great deal of time communicating.

Little did I realize that in just a week's time, I would find a meaningful parallel in my relationship with the Lord. I had set out on a trip to Wyoming and Nebraska to coordinate some early morning seminaries. After taking care of some business in Cheyenne, I got back into my little Volkswagen and headed west toward Scottsbluff, Nebraska. It was a beautiful night—a few low clouds were scooting along, and the moon was almost full. I made it a practice while driving alone over such long distances to pray vocally—it was a great way to spend my time and it was always so spiritually stimulating. In fact, some of the greatest spiritual experiences I've had have occurred while pouring out my heart in prayer as I drove alone.

This particular evening as I lifted my voice in prayer, my thoughts turned completely to my dad. There flooded into my mind and heart many beautiful memories of experiences I had had with him and I found myself not only reviewing, but in a sense reliving, specific experiences that were among the choicest of those memories. As I seemingly relived those experiences, I felt profoundly of my father's presence. There came with tremendous intensity feelings of love and appreciation for him, convincing evidence to me that such love was a gift of God. I felt equally impressed that I received that experience as a motivation to do all in my power to be sure I could obtain the promise of being with him forever.

I arrived in Scottsbluff quite late and stayed with some Saints. The following morning while I was preparing for breakfast, the phone rang. It was a long distance call for me, and I learned that during the night my father had very unexpectedly passed away.

As I hung up the phone, there immediately came into my mind the beautiful experience I had had in talking to Dad just one week before. How grateful I was that we had opened our hearts so totally to each other and had shared so deeply our love for each other.

Then, the experience the night before took on even greater meaning. I felt the Lord had prepared me for my father's passing by allowing me to feel so deeply of his presence and so deeply of the love that bound us together. I count that evening as one of the greatest experiences of my life. How profoundly grateful I am for the principle of prayer and for the reality of the love, comfort, and strength of the Savior.

But of necessity I have to conclude that I don't believe I ever would have had that experience with Dad a week before he died had we not spent a great deal of time talking with each other, nor would I have had the veil-thinning experience I had the night of his death had I not been so motivated by the prophets to pray mightily and persistently to my heavenly Father in the name of Christ.

Knowing Christ Through Prayer to the Father

The Savior has given a divine sequence on our knowing him first and the Father second: "No man knoweth the Son, but the Father; neither knoweth any man the Father, save the Son, and he to whomsoever the Son will reveal him." (Matthew 11:27.) Yet we are commanded to pray to the Father in the name of Christ (3 Nephi 18:19). How can we get to know the Lord if we don't pray directly to him?

Perhaps the answer is found in the following ideas: We acknowledge that it is the Father, even Elohim, who provided for us a Redeemer in Christ. It is the Father's plan of redemption, not Christ's; however, we call upon the Father in the name of the Son because the Son provided the possibility of our actual redemption from the fall. He, the Son, suffered for us, died for us, and broke the bands of death for us, thereby earning the right and title of our advocate with the Father (D&C 45:3) and the only mediator between God and man (1 Timothy 2:5). Because the Savior is our mediator, our prayers go through Christ to the Father, and the Father answers our prayers through his Son.

I think a classic example of this idea is found in the First Vision. As Joseph read the promise of the apostle James (James 1:4-5), the Spirit bore such a powerful witness to him that the promise was true that he immediately went out into the forest and lifted his voice in prayer to Heavenly Father. In answer to his prayer, both the Father and the Son appeared to him. But interestingly enough, all the Father did was introduce his Son and invite Joseph to "hear him." Joseph's prayer was actually answered by the Savior.

Consider a second example that has to do with our receiving any spiritual endowment or blessing. For instance, suppose we seek mightily for a remission of sins, acknowledging that it is the Savior who made available the means by which we might be freed from our sins. It is Heavenly Father we ask explicitly and in the name of Christ that we might through our faith in Christ obtain that blessed gift. If our faith is sufficient and our repentance complete, the Father responds to our prayers by having his Son cleanse and sanctify us. By the time we are sanctified and made clean, we, like thousands of others, testify of the reality and goodness of Christ and we feel a profound relationship of a personal nature with him.

As we, like the prophets, call upon the Father in the name of Christ and increase in our reception of personal revelation, we will come out of our private chambers, off the mountains, or out of the deserts testifying of the living reality of Christ and of his intervention in our lives. Initially it may seem difficult to understand how it is that as we call upon the Father in the name of Christ, we will be introduced in a marvelous way to the Savior. But it is a true principle, and one that we will understand more fully as we experience it.

Letting the Spirit Teach You How to Pray

One of the reasons the Jews criticized the Savior was that he told them that if they would do his will, that is, keep his commandments, they would know he was the Son of God. However, they wanted to know without question he was the Son of God *before* keeping his commandments. People often approach prayer in the same way. They want to know before they pray that the Lord will help them pray in the way they should and that he will answer their prayers. Actually, they will never receive his help unless they start calling upon him night and day in the best way they know how.

I don't know of any more effective way to learn to pray than just to pray. We learn how to swim by getting in the water and practicing and practicing. We learn how to ski and perform every other physical skill by doing and doing. And so it is with prayer. If we set aside a long enough period each day that will stretch us and push us and if we strive consistently with it, the Lord will send his Spirit to teach us how to pray.

To learn to pray, then, requires some tremendous effort on our part, and if we persist, we will come to the point where we know our prayers are being heard, where we know we are making contact with heaven. But, ironically enough, it is not unusual, once we know we can make contact, once we know he is blessing us in our prayers, to be so satisfied with that knowledge that we don't continue to persist! It is about the price we have to pay to continue to grow in our contact with the Lord through prayer that I would like to make some observations.

The Labor of Prayer

On one occasion I was having lunch with a family in El Paso. They had a young son who was quite a gifted pianist. I asked him, "John, how much time do you spend practicing the piano?" He responded without hesitation, "Approximately five hours a day." I thought, "What a price to pay to develop his musical talent!"

I have observed over the years the tremendous price students will pay to obtain their degrees, excell in debate or athletics, or achieve anything else they really desire. There is no question that the law of the harvest is real and applies to everything we do in life. If we want to reap a bounteous harvest, we must cultivate a bounteous crop. And so it is with prayer. If we really want to continue to make contact with and obtain the powers of heaven, we've got to put a great deal of time and effort into prayer.

When I returned home from my mission, there was no question that my spiritual appetite had been whetted by my experience in the field, and I was determined to keep the spiritual generators humming. However, what a challenge it was to switch from missionary work to spending almost every waking moment working in the fields! It was hard to feel I was growing spiritually even though I was attending my meetings, doing my church work, and searching the scriptures. I felt that there was surely something else I could do and must do—a greater price I needed to pay—that would assure me of continued spiritual growth and development.

As I looked desperately for a practical formula that, if applied regularly, would assure me of the growth and development I desired, I commenced rereading the Book of Mormon. As I read, I was especially impressed by the experience of Enos, son of Jacob. It seemed, in fact, as if he were speaking directly to me, and the conversation in my mind went something like this:

"George, how many times have you read this little book I wrote?"

"Oh, maybe ten or fifteen times. Why?"

"Have you ever tried doing what I did?"

"You mean pray all day and into the night?"

"Yes."

"My goodness, no!"

"Well, why do you think I wrote the book?"

"Oh, you mean you wrote the book to show that that's the kind of price you have to pay in prayer to really break through?"

"Yes, yes, you're really sharp. After reading the book ten or fifteen times, it finally dawns on you why I wrote it—that is, after I told you!"

I then seemed to receive a personal challenge from Enos: "George, why don't you go into the mountains and pray all day and into the night?"

"Hey," I thought, "that's a great idea!"

I got excited and determined that that was what I would do. I made arrangements so my chores could be done by someone else, and set aside a whole day and a night for my big experience.

It was a beautiful summer day, and as I drove as high as I could on the highest mountain around and then hiked way above timberline to the very top, I was about as excited as I'd ever been. I just knew this was going to be the biggest day of my life—that surely I would rend the veil and receive a remission of my sins. I said to myself, "Undoubtedly, when I'm through today they will want to change the name of the mountains from Mount Harrison to Mount Sinai!" In fact, I was confident that by the time I got off the mountain, there would be a new little book in the Book of Mormon called the "Book of George."

I found a place right on the very top where I could kneel by a flat rock and support part of my weight by leaning on it. (I wanted to be reasonably comfortable because I was going to be there a long time!) Knowing I was alone, that no one was around for miles, and having everything in readiness, I tilted back my head and really lifted my voice to the heavens. As I did, the image of Enos and Nephi and other prophets in the attitude of prayer came into my mind and I was quite pleased with what I was doing.

However, much to my amazement, after roughly twenty minutes I completely ran out of things to say! Even at that, I had been a little repetitious! I felt totally chagrined that I was through so soon and couldn't think of one more thing to say. After a few more minutes, I got up off my knees, hiked down to the car, and drove home. On the way, I guess because I was so shocked and disappointed at not being able to pray for more than twenty minutes, I started rationalizing (to rationalize is to bring one's ideals down to one's conduct). The first thing I thought was, "Enos, you must have really been a sinner! It took you all day and into the night and after twenty minutes I feel fine! Not only that, do you know how many widows you could have visited in a day and a night, and how much scripture you could have read in that much time, and how many potatoes you could have picked on the welfare farm?" But the real clincher was this thought: "Enos, do you know how many ward and stake leaders I know who have never prayed for more than twenty minutes? So there!"

But despite my rationalization, by the time I drove into the farm yard and turned the key off in the car I was emotionally wiped out—so disappointed. I sat in the car for some time, feeling convinced that there must be a way to develop sufficient spiritual starch in one's spine to pay the kind of price that not only Enos paid, but in my estimation all the prophets paid; a price that would enable one to say, "I have conversed with my God as one man converses with another!"

That day (and this is what made the whole experience so worthwhile), I determined to set aside sufficient time each day for my verbal prayers to require the real exercise of faith; enough time that would demand some real reaching and struggling so that the spiritual fibers of my being would be greatly exercised and hopefully become strong. I determined that 15 or 20 minutes a day would accomplish that exercise, and I made a commitment that I would spend at least that much time in prayer each day.

In the ensuing days and weeks as I tried to stick with my commitment, I found I had been right! The 15 or 20 minutes a day was more than enough time to really stretch my spiritual faculties. In fact, I was literally stunned at how hard it was to pray consistently for that much time each day! It was hard emotionally as well as physically. It was much easier to read the scriptures regularly and to do my church work consistently (both of which I continued doing), but so very hard to subdue my body and lift my voice in verbal prayer. I would stay with my commitment for a period of time, but then because of the many pressures of family responsibilities, church callings, earning a living and so forth, I'd quit doing it for a while. However, as I reflected on what I honestly wanted to achieve in life, invariably the desire to communicate more fully in prayer would return with increased intensity, and I would pick up my challenge again.

Even though I was inconsistent in my efforts, I realized that something was beginning to happen. I sensed that my appetite for the things of the Spirit was increasing. I became aware of a deeper feeling of optimism about life. I felt a closer affinity for the Lord. Little bits of inspiration started coming that really made a difference in my life. It was hard to put my finger right on it, but some exciting feelings were coming. While many times I still had to push myself to keep the commitment to pray for 15 to 20 minutes a day, over a period of several months it started to become an important part of my life. Again, it still took some pushing and struggling to maintain a consistent pattern, but by now the benefits were so obvious, the blessings so much greater than I had ever enjoyed, that my devotion to and consistency with prayer became an integral part of my daily life and the very highlight of each day.

I have become convinced that when we persist in prayer, our spirits are actually exercising their muscles, becoming strong, becoming prepared, so that as the gates of revelation gradually start opening (and invariably it will be very gradual), we will have the strength and the courage to accept and implement the ideas and directions that are coming. The Lord is so kind and gracious to us that he generally won't give us more light and knowledge than we can handle, but when he becomes convinced of the sincerity of our hearts as evidenced by our determination to knock and knock and knock, he will see that our prayers are not in vain.

Persistence, effort, and determination to really make contact with the powers of heaven in order to communicate with God as one man converses with another will pay off in dividends and blessings greater than one can imagine. The veil will become thin and even nonexistent, and we will receive—oh, I know that is true!

Becoming Filled With Desire

I stood one spring on Mars Hill in Athens, Greece, and as I looked across a small valley to the Acropolis where the remains of the famous Parthenon stood, there came into my mind a story told about Socrates, the famous Greek philosopher. It appears a young man came to Socrates and inquired as to how he could obtain the knowledge Socrates possessed. The young man was invited by the great philosopher to follow him, and they walked until they came to a river. Without pausing, Socrates walked out to where the water was chest high, and the young man followed. Socrates grabbed the inquirer, plunged him under the water and held him there until he passed out. He then dragged him to the shore and let him lie.

When the young man came to and his strength returned, he sought out Socrates again and asked, "Why did you do that? I almost lost my life!"

Socrates replied, "While you were under the water, what did you want more than anything else?"

The young man answered, "Air."

Socrates said, "As soon as you want knowledge as much as you wanted air, nothing on the face of the earth can keep you from getting it!"

A similar point was brought home to me once as I was lecturing in San Fernando, California. I was really pleading with the Saints to take the time and effort to pray when this thought entered my mind: "George, had you been willing to spend one-fifth of the time reaching for the things of the Spirit that you spent practicing and playing high school football, you could have been translated by the time you were 19!" At that moment there flooded into my memory the intense desire I had while in high school to play football. It had been an obsession with me; I was willing to run great distances, scrimmage for hours, do calisthenics—I ate, drank, and slept football, so to speak, and it paid off. I got to be on the team all through my high school years.

It is true that our desires determine the very course and destiny of our lives. We can tell easily enough if we want something by whether or not we get it. If we really desire righteousness, we will receive it. In quite a real sense, on judgment day, we will receive exactly what we lived and worked for. If the verdict given us is less than celestial glory, the Lord won't send an unusually strong angel to come and carry us screaming and protesting wildly to the terrestrial or telestial kingdom. We will be pleased to accept quietly the verdict and go to our assigned place because again, we will receive exactly according to our desires.

The ability to persist in our prayers is actually a gift of God! Only the Lord finally can endow us with the strength to pay a consistent price in mighty prayer and he does it by giving us the desire. In no other place is this idea more effectively taught than in the experience of the twelve disciples when "they did still continue, without ceasing, to pray unto him; and they did not multiply many words, for it was given unto them what they should pray, and they were filled with desire." (3 Nephi 19:24; see also Romans 8:26, Jude 20, and D&C 50:29-30.) Why were they placed in a position to persist as they did? Because, I believe, the Spirit took over and gave them the desire.

The Lord is so gracious! Knowing our fallen nature, he sends mighty men of God in our midst (Moroni 7:31-32) to testify in power of the greater blessings that are available. Because of their witness, righteous desires are planted and stirred up in our hearts. Not only are we influenced by the testimonies of others, but it is important to realize that we are agents unto ourselves. If we don't have the desire to pray, all we have to do is ask for the desire! We have enough control over our minds and bodies to dictate to ourselves, to tell our bodies to kneel and our tongue to ask for righteous desires, and lo and behold, the Lord will give those desires to us. Again, if we ask, if we persist, our desires in righteousness will grow and grow and become the well-spring of eternal life.

The following experience might be helpful in showing how the Lord will give us the ability to pray with fervor by filling us with desire.

One morning in the early hours, I was going where I like to go for my personal devotionals. It was quite cold, and because of a night's rest that had been far too brief, I felt extremely tired. I wondered if I just ought to collapse into a ball and roll back down the mountain into bed. In fact, about the only thing that kept coming into my mind as I walked along so dreary-eyed was "retire to thy bed early, that ye may not be weary." (D&C 88:124) However, I pushed on to where I like to go and knelt in prayer for ten or fifteen minutes. The words were hard to come by and when they did come, they seemed listless and without power. But I persisted, and then it came—the quiet assurance that I was being heard—and I felt such a strong desire to pray, to make contact, to come alive in His spirit and power. Ideas started coming. I became so excited about the new day dawning and the opportunities it presented that I was physically rejuvinated. After a half an hour or so had passed, I jumped up off my knees and ran all the way down to the house. I was ready for an exciting day, knowing I had really conversed with my maker.

When the Heavens Seem Like Brass

One reason we may find it hard to persist in mighty prayer is that much of the time our prayers are not answered while we are asking them. A General Authority once told how, when faced with a particular challenge, he fasted one day a week and sought help in fervent prayer each day for a year before the answer came. Often decisions must be made, presented to the Lord, and the process of carrying them out commenced before the full confirmation comes that the decision was correct. In these instances and many more that could be cited, evidence is ample that the challenge is great and one's faith is really tested when answers do not come quickly and the heavens seem like brass, although the prayers continue to ascend to heaven.

Perhaps another reason the heavens might seem like brass is because we often do not recognize answers when they come. We might be looking for the spectacular and miss the quiet increase of peace, confidence, and optimism that is coming into our hearts.

Another reason persistence may be hard is that some of the time while we are praying, the Spirit will actually withdraw from us. How difficult it is to continue to cry unto God when the Spirit is not there! But again, there has to be a great reason why this happens. Is there a greater challenge to our faith than to pray persistently when the Spirit is withdrawn? I think not. To show what I mean, let me describe an experience that particularly illustrates this point.

Eleven years after my attempt to play Enos, I was in the little hamlet of Rye, Colorado, which sits quite high on the eastern slope of the Rockies, twenty or thirty miles south of Pueblo. I visited an early morning seminary class and thrilled with the spirit of a great teacher who had every LDS high school youth in class, plus several non-members. When the class concluded, I drove up the valley to the end of the road and obtained permission from a rancher to hike up the mountains above his ranch. It was wintertime, and although there was quite a bit of snow on the ground, it was warm and comfortable on the sunny side of the mountain. As I climbed higher and higher, I felt a very strong desire to obtain more power from the Lord that I might be a better husband and a better father. I wanted to be much more effective in magnifying my callings in the Priesthood. I desired a greater ability to teach the gospel with the Spirit, to have the convincing power of God, that I might particularly be able to touch the lives of the inactive LDS youth at Colorado State University.

Finally, I located the place I wanted to spend the day—it was next to a large fallen tree. I knelt and prayed for an hour and was surprised that the Spirit didn't come as I was used to feeling it. I continued another hour and another, but still no quiet assurance that He was there and listening. However, in spite of what appeared to be a lack of the Spirit, with some determination I persisted in vocal prayer throughout the entire day. Much to my distress, the heavens indeed were like brass. To persist that day in vocal prayer ended up being the hardest, most difficult, challenging experience of my entire life, emotionally, physically, and spiritually. I knew what it was to work hard on the farm. I had had the experience of bucking potatoes for 20 hours straight; I had thinned sugar beets all day long in the hot sun to the point where I wondered if my back would allow me ever to walk in an upright position again. But none of these experiences taxed my endurance like praying all day long high on a mountain above Rye, Colorado.

About evening I concluded my prayers, worked my way off the mountain and drove back to Fort Collins. While driving back, I felt exhausted, discouraged, and honestly wondered if I had wasted the whole day. I also wondered if I were a fanatic to desire so intently the greater blessings and endowments that seemed so consistently promised in the scriptures.

However, over the next few weeks, interesting things began to occur. The day after my experience on the mountain as I put my arms around my wife and held her close, and then held my children one by one, I felt a greater intensity of love for them than I had ever felt before. Throughout the next several weeks as I knocked on fraternity and sorority doors and invited inactive young men and women to come and participate in the Lord's program, I felt the convincing power of God greater than I had ever felt it. It seemed to me that as I opened the scriptures, everywhere I looked I saw the majesty of the Savior and his infinite atonement. For weeks I felt a greater outpouring of the Spirit than during any previous period in my life. What a blessing that day of prayer was to me. How grateful I was that even though throughout the entire day I did not feel his Spirit, I stayed and persisted in prayer.

Repititious Prayers

Just a comment about the problem of repetition in prayer—obviously, the Lord doesn't want us to use vain repetitions (Matthew 6:7). But by vain repetition does the Lord mean prayers in which we ask for the same thing again and again? Does he mean prayers that are uttered too often or are too lengthy? I don't think so. I think the Lord is referring to prayers that are not uttered sincerely or with real intent.

The Lord's parable of the importunate widow (Luke 18:1-7) is an excellent case in point, illustrating how one should be willing to persist and persist in prayer. The parable tells of a certain widow who kept approaching a judge to avenge her of her adversary. The widow kept persisting to the point where her continued requests were wearying the judge. Finally the judge, although he "feared not God, neither regarded man," responded to the widow's request. Having a loving Savior as we do, how much more willing is he to respond to our persistent requests. The following analogy might serve further to illustrate. Suppose you are swimming in a river with a friend. After a while you climb out on the bank to rest. While you are watching your friend, you become alarmed to hear him frantically calling, "Help! Help!" He disappears beneath the water for a few moments, but upon reappearing again yells, "Help! Help!" As you hear him cry for help the second time, I doubt very much that you would say, "I'm sorry, dear friend, but you requested help the second time in exactly the same manner as you requested help the first time, which is a sure indication that you don't really need or want help!" We might on different occasions ask again and again and again for particular blessings; however, we will not be guilty of vain repetitions if we really desire that which we pray for.

What to Pray For and About

As we continue trying to become more effective in our prayers, it's helpful to have in mind many different things about which we would like to approach the Lord. Then, as we pray, we may feel impressed by the Spirit to pray more fervently about one thing than another. A partial list of things to pray about could include expressing appreciation for our blessings, with a particular emphasis on the life and mission of the Savior, and the restored Church; we should feel free to pray for the temporal blessings we need to accomplish—all the things we feel the Lord would have us accomplish; we ought to seek diligently for the constant companionship of the Holy Ghost; we should persist in prayer for charity, the pure love of Christ. It is also important to exercise our faith in prayer for the General Authorities and all who are laboring in the cause of Zion. We should pray that the Lord will soften the hearts of the leaders of the nations of the earth that they might allow the missionaries into their countries.

In addition, I would like to mention several other areas about which we should pray to the Lord and elaborate on them in some detail because they seem to represent some special concerns and challenges.

Pray to Acquire Faith

I think it is obvious that *the* purpose of prayer is to increase our faith in the Savior. The more we learn about him, the more experiences we have with him, and the more we understand his mind and will, the greater will be our faith in him.

I would like to stress that the quickest way to acquire a mighty faith is through prayer. To illustrate, let's return to the experience of Enos. Enos had gone to hunt animals, but he began to reflect on his relationship with the Lord and determined to obtain a remission of his sins. He testified, "all the day long did I cry unto him; yea, and when the night came I did still raise my voice high that it reached the heavens." (Enos 4.)

Let's imagine that Enos started praying sometime in the early morning. By noon he hadn't received a remission of his sins, nor had he by the late afternoon. (Incidentally it is my personal opinion that Enos surely must have prayed many times before the experience to have had the spiritual stamina needed to persist as he did.) But Enos continued with great determination, and sometime late that night, or perhaps even in the early hours of the next morning, Enos heard the voice of the Lord and received a remission of sins. Over a period of a day and night, Enos, through his struggle in mighty prayer, obtained enough faith to hear the voice of the Lord and receive a remission of sins. What a correlation between his persistence in prayer and the faith he enjoyed!

Pray for Loved Ones

How important it is to pray for our loved ones. "Pray one for another," counseled the apostle James, for "the effectual fervent prayer of a righteous man availeth much." (James 5:16) And even though we ourselves are weak and fall short in many ways of being the individuals we should be, the Lord nevertheless hears our prayers in behalf of our loved ones.

One New Year's day, I determined to commence the new year by putting forth a special effort in early morning prayer. It was several hours before dawn, and the ground was quite heavily blanketed with snow. The lights from the city reflected off the snow, and as I looked down from quite high on the mountain, it was indeed a beautiful sight.

I persisted for a period of time in prayer, and after mentioning those things I generally pray about, I found my attention turning to my beloved brothers and sisters. I found myself caught up in unusually powerful feelings of love for each of them, and I lifted my voice in their behalf. Words are so inadequate to express the feelings that came for my brothers and sisters on that occasion, and for quite a length of time I continued to pray for their welfare.

After concluding my prayers, I returned home, awakened the family, and we began to prepare for a New Year's dinner to which we had invited one of my brothers and his family.

Later that day, following dinner, most of the children had left the table and I felt strongly impressed to lean toward my brother and ask him if I could give him a special priesthood blessing. I felt bold in asking, but his instantaneous response removed any apprehension I had. He, his wife, their invalid daughter and I slipped into the bedroom.

The blessing given came from above and was a special experience between two brothers. At the conclusion of that blessing, it seemed so natural to ask if his wife would appreciate a blessing. She, too, was so responsive, and again the kindness of the Lord was manifest. Then, at the daughter's request, I was able to bless her.

At the end of the day, our loved ones having returned home, Diane and I had retired and were lying in bed, both quite subdued by the beauty of that day. My wife said, among other things, "I don't know when we have had a more beautiful day with relatives than we had today." I felt in my heart a special appreciation for the many prophets who encourage us so effectively to make prayer for others an important part of our lives.

Some months later my brother called long distance and indicated that he had returned to the temple after an absence of some time. How I thrilled at this, and knew again that the Lord blesses our loved ones in response to our prayers for them.

Pray For Comfort

We are assured that we can have peace in this world in spite of the challenges and difficulties that come our way. The Lord has promised us the Comforter to assist us through sorrows, grief, and heartaches, but again, prayer is the key to that peace and comfort.

At one time in my life, I arrived at a point where I was unusually discouraged. It seemed so difficult to do all the things that I felt were expected of me, and I really wondered if it was all worth it. I remember going to where I like to pray, wondering if I even wanted to ask for encouragement and comfort. I knelt and prayed for some time, specifically about the heavy burdens that seemed to be mine, and then enjoyed the following delightful experience. Incidentally, I might add that the Lord works with all of us according to our particular needs and experiences. He also draws from our experiences to teach us great lessons—such was the case this day with me.

It seemed that all of a sudden, I was on a football field, and all the feelings I had as a high school football player seemed to return—the crisp fall air of Southern Idaho, the sound of the high school band, the excitement of having my parents watching, and the thrill that comes in anticipation of the kickoff—it was all there and all so real.

Finally, the whistle blew, the ball was kicked, and I caught it. I immediately started running down the field to try to make a touchdown. Discouragement number one: as I looked for the goal posts, they appeared to be about a mile away. I had never seen such a long football field! I wondered if I could even run that far, let alone fight my way through the opposing team!

Then I became aware of the opposing team. It looked like there were at least eighteen men, and I thought, "Wait a minute, this isn't right, there are only supposed to be eleven—and not only that, they don't all have to be 300 pounds!" That was discouragement number two. But when excitement gets the adrenalin working anything seems possible, and in spite of the odds, I kept running as fast as I could. As I ran, the comforting thought came that my team would surely run interference for me. So while continuing to run, I looked to the right and to the left—discouragement number three: I was the only one on my team!

Oh, I'll never forget the feeling of utter hopelessness that came then. I just knew there was no way I could make a touchdown. In fact, I felt if I were smart, I would throw the ball away and just sit down—anything to stop what was an impossible situation! But right at that moment of greatest discouragement, I became aware that there were individuals lined up on both sides of the field—it seemed they were the prophets from Adam to Spencer W. Kimball. They were giving words of great encouragement, telling me to keep going, to give it all I had, not to let down, telling me that there wasn't anything I was asked to do but what the Lord would give me the power to do it if I would look to him.

Then the experience was over, but I came away with a comfort and a determination to continue to try with all of my heart to do what I know is expected of me. That experience was a significant source of motivation and encouragement, and I know it came as a result of my seeking comfort from the Lord in prayer.

The Challenge

What if we were to discover that of all the important things that we need to do to qualify ourselves for ultimate exaltation, the one thing that will do the most to enable us to do everything else, is mighty prayer? And further, that the one thing that will enable our prayers to be truly mighty is praying long enough each day to demand a real effort, a real exercise of faith? And finally, that twenty or thirty minutes a day in verbal prayer, if persisted in, will put us in contact with the powers we need, to become all the Lord would like us to become? Surely, if we discovered such truths, would we not be pleased to take advantage of them?

It seems as though there exists an invisible barrier that keeps us initially from accomplishing different goals that are really challenging. As an example, to break into a consistent pattern of running or jogging initially requires some strenuous effort on the part of almost everyone, but once the body is conditioned, how enjoyable running can be. To develop the ability to do difficult routines in gymnastics demands overcoming fear and developing never before used muscles, but again, once those barriers are broken, the thrilling satisfaction of successfully doing challenging routines is difficult to describe. To learn how to fast effectively requires a cleansing of the body that for the first several serious fasts is somewhat uncomfortable, if not quite painful. But once the body is cleansed, a barrier is cleared and fasting can be a beautiful experience and remarkably rewarding spiritually.

It is no different with prayer. In order to arrive at a point where "mighty prayer" (D&C 29:1-2) is an integral part of one's daily life, it seems as though there is a barrier to break, an initial struggle required, but once the barrier is broken, the blessings of mighty prayer are inestimable.

It is possible to know a great deal about religion and not necessarily live our lives in harmony with what we know. It isn't too difficult to be "hearers of the word," but it is a great challenge to be "doers of the word." (James 1:22.) Something that has caused me some serious concern and has caused me to stress the importance of prayer is the discovery that not very many students among those whom I have taught were currently investing nor had they ever invested very much time in prayer! It was uncommon to discover individuals who had reached beyond the perfunctory saying of their prayers. It was very rare to discover those who had ever prayed for thirty minutes, let alone an hour. Again, these discoveries caused me to want to stress mighty prayer, to plead with the students to set aside sufficient time to lift up their voices in mighty prayer even as they set aside so many minutes to search the scriptures or to do other things. As a result, I have challenged my students over the years to pray for twenty or thirty minutes a day for a month, that they might break the "prayer barrier," that they might begin to taste what mighty prayer is all about.

The challenge to pray for twenty or thirty minutes a day has produced more results in terms of spiritual growth and development in the lives of those who seriously implemented the challenge than any other challenge I have given. There seems to be something almost magical about twenty or thirty minutes of vocal daily prayer. There is something that happens when one struggles and pleads for that long. There is a stretching of one's spiritual fibers that causes them to grow; there is a concentration demanded that pulls on the stuff real faith is made of; there is a gradual infusion into one's spine of spiritual starch that really propels one to seek, hunger, thirst, and strive for righteousness. One can't pray for twenty or thirty minutes a day but what it pushes one beyond the mechanical aspects of prayer into the prayer of real faith, which invariably brings greater and greater knowledge and power from the Lord.

I would encourage you with all of my heart to accept the challenge to pray for twenty or thirty minutes a day. If you will do it diligently, you will begin to taste of some powers and feelings that will give you the confidence that life is not only worthwhile, but that you can and will ultimately receive everything that the Father and the Son have. It is hard to break the prayer barrier, but you can do it, and once you do break that barrier, you will find mighty prayer such an integral part of your life that it will be a daily experience that will be as natural and spontaneous as breathing.

I believe there can be an advantage in having a special place and a special time for our personal prayers. To keep a period of the day hallowed and to have a place which becomes especially sacred is to build a meaningful tradition that will become a great source of strength. We may choose to set aside the early hours of the day, noon, or late at night; we may go to a bedroom, a furnace room, a grove of trees or a mountain—a time and place where we can turn our thoughts and attention to the sacred experience of prayer.

Prayer Unlocks the Doors of Heaven

Is it any wonder, then, that prayer is seen by many as the very key to a knowledge of God? The first step to eternal life? The connecting link between God and man? The message of the prophets of all ages is that we can converse with the Lord and obtain from him the knowledge and ability to live by faith. How powerfully and beautifully the prophet Joseph Smith said it when he declared, "It is the first principle of the gospel to know for a certainty the character of God and that we may converse with him as one man converses with another." (*TPJS*, p. 345.)

What a meaningful principle! I know that it's true! As with the development of any Christlike quality, it takes a great deal of determination and persistence to have our prayers become meaningful on a daily basis. But, as the truth of that principle is burned into your soul by the witness of the Spirit and you grow and persist in mighty prayer, your experiences in prayer will be the greatest source of spiritual motivation in your life, and you will in time come to converse with the Father in the name of Christ as one man converses with another!

I know God hears and answers prayers and that under the quiet whisperings of the Holy Ghost and through other means, he can and will bless us with our every need. Conversing with God is the means by which we acquire a personal relationship with the Lord. As we grow in the spirit and power of prayer, the reality of the Savior, his atonement, and his revelations through mighty prophets of God will be the anchor and the strength of our lives.

Chapter 3

To Know The Lord Is To Know He Is Literally The Son Of God

The most important, basic doctrine of true Christianity—that doctrine which gives birth to, upholds, supports and sustains the entire structure of the plan of salvation—is that Jesus Christ is literally divine, the offspring of Diety. Without a belief in the divinity of Christ as taught abundantly in the scriptures and through the words of living prophets, Christianity loses its image of divinity. Consequently, like all other religions and vain philosophies of man's wisdom, it becomes nothing more than a mere system of ethics.

The scriptures contain many beautiful testimonies of the literal Sonship of Christ. In the Book of Mormon, Nephi, after having been shown the vision of the tree of life which his father had seen, asked for an interpretation of that vision. As the interpretation was given, Nephi saw a "virgin most beautiful and fair above all virgins," and he was told by an angel that she was "the mother of the Son of God, after the manner of the flesh." This virgin whom Nephi saw was carried away in the Spirit for a space of time, then appeared bearing a child in her arms. The angel declared, "Behold the Lamb of God, yea, even the Son of the Eternal Father!" (1 Nephi 11:15, 18, 21.)

The New Testament accounts that Jesus was begotten of the Father by Mary are equally clear and should leave no question in the minds of those filled with the Spirit that Jesus is the literal offspring of God our Heavenly Father.

Perhaps one of the most powerful declarations of the divine Sonship of Christ is Joseph's inspired witness:

> And now, after the many testimonies which have been given of him, this is the testimony, last of all, which we give of him: that he lives! For we saw him, even on the right hand of God; and we heard the voice bearing record that he is the only begotten of the Father. (D&C 76:22-23.)

Melvin J. Ballard bore a beautiful testimony of the Savior's literal Sonship:

> One of the great questions that I have referred to that the world is concerned about, and is in confusion over, is as to whether or not his was a virgin birth, a birth wherein divine power interceded. Joseph Smith made it perfectly clear that Jesus Christ told the absolute truth, as did those who testify concerning him, the Apostles of the Lord Jesus Christ, wherein he is declared to be the very Son of God. And if God the Eternal Father is not the real Father of Jesus Christ, then are we in confusion; then is he not in reality the Son of God. But we declare that he is the Only Begotten of the Father in the flesh.
>
> Mary told the story most beautifully when she said that an angel of the Lord came to her and told her that she had found favor in the sight of God, and had come to be

worthy of the fulfillment of the promises heretofore made, to become the virgin mother of the Redeemer of the world. She afterwards, referring to the event, said: "God hath done wonderful things unto me." "And the Holy Ghost came upon her," is the story, "and she came into the presence of the highest." No man or woman can live in mortality and survive the presence of the Highest except by the sustaining power of the Holy Ghost. So it came upon her to prepare her for admittance into the divine presence, and the power of the Highest, who is the Father, was present, and overshadowed her, and the holy child that was born of her was called the Son of God. (Melvin J. Ballard, *Deseret News, Church Section,* September 19, 1936, pp. 2, 8.)

Probably one of the most beautiful accounts that portrays the sanctity, beauty, and reality of the Savior's divine birth is the following account by Elder S. Dilworth Young:

As Told By James, Of This Elder Brother
JESUS CHRIST, THE SON OF GOD

What I am about to say and the manner of its saying is in response to a request made by those who planned this program. Some of the things I shall mention are based on the accepted accounts; some are imaginary. You will recognize each of these without further comment from me. What liberties I have taken with established texts are also easily recognized and need no explanation. However, I should like to tell you that I shall take liberty with two proper names in the sense that I have chosen to use these names in English as derived from the Aramaic tongue, the language spoken by the Jews at the time of Christ, rather than from the Greek from which these names usually come down to you. I shall have to make myself somebody else. You will forgive me for that.

* * * * * * * * * *

Let me introduce myself as being James. I have four brothers. Jeshua is the oldest—my elder brother. Joses, Simon, Judas are my younger brothers. I have three sisters.

We lived quite simply in a little town called Nazareth. We had to live simply. My father was a carpenter. The carpenter's trade was dull business in our town. We made furniture as needed by the townspeople; we repaired furniture; we built houses; and we built stables and other shelter.

As small boys we often sat upon the roof of our house in the cool of the evening, and we would ask mother and father for stories. One story we liked especially well was how the angel came to each house in Mizraim and spared the first-born of those houses that were marked with the blood of the sacrificial lamb. Then we liked, too, how our people were in the wilderness, they were fed manna.

I asked my mother, "What is manna?"

She said, "I do not know, only that they were told that they must gather only enough for the day, for if they took more, it would spoil."

And the story of how the quails miraculously became food for them when they were desperately hungry. Those stories brought the ancient customs of our people to my mind.

But our favorite story was the one about the time when Father and Mother and Jeshua went to live in Mizraim shortly after Jeshua was born; how when they had no money, some men from the East had visited them and had given them gold and frankincense and myrrh as a birth gift to Jeshua. She told how they had said that they had followed a star to our door.

We would ask, "Was Jeshua born in a stable?"

Mother would say, "Yes, but when these men came, we had moved from the stable into a house. It had been several days before we could obtain the lodgings, but your father searched and finally found a place."

"Was there a star?"

Mother said, "I did not see it, but the men said that a star showed them which way to go and indicated where to find us."

"Why did you go to Mizraim?"

"An angel came and warned us," said my father, "to leave and not come back until we were told, so we felt we needed to obey. It was fortunate for us that the men gave us gifts, for with the gold, we purchased asses to go to Mizraim—four of them, and with the money from the sale of the frankincense and the myrrh, we lived in Mizraim until it was safe to come home."

And how excited I became when my mother told me about the great sandstorm which they met on the way, which so suddenly came up that they could not pitch their little tent. How they were enveloped in the terrible wind and darkness of blowing and drifting sand. They struggled on and fortunately fell into, literally, a caravan with tents pitched and safe. The caravan leaders took them in, preserved them; and, from then on, they accompanied the caravan to Mizraim. Those were our favorite stories as we would sit on the roof of our house looking up at the stars.

Daily we learned our trade. Father was a hard taskmaster in the sense that he insisted that we learn—that is, all but Jeshua. He had liberty. He used to take long walks alone. Sometimes, as we grew older, He would be gone two or three nights; and Mother would worry about Him. Father, upon His return, never rebuked Him.

I would hear him say, "Jeshua, was your trip fruitful?"

"Yes, Father."

"Did you find what you sought?"

"I found fourfold," He would reply.

It is easy now, looking back, to see what He meant. I think our friend, Matthew, who wrote so extensively of His life, truly said He "grew up with his brethren, and waxed strong, and waited upon the Lord for the time of his ministry to come. And he served under his father, and he spake not as other men, neither could he be taught; for he needed not that any man should teach him." (Inspired Version, Matthew 3:24, 25.)

It was on THAT day—that day when Mother prepared a special feast for us. She had procured a lamb and cooked it with vegetables into a most tasty dish. When we were through eating, Jeshua arose, kissed his sisters, embraced Father and each of us, and gave honor especially to Mother and said good-by.

"The time has come, Mother. I am thankful to you for being my mother—and to you, Father, for your care of me."

Later we asked Mother why He must leave, and she said: "He is going to His work. God, His Father, has called Him."

"What work?"

"I cannot tell you. I am not quite sure myself. I know only that He is to save the people. I have not told you before, but now you should know that when He was born, an angel commanded your father to name Him "Jeshua," "The Anointed One." The angel told your father that He was born to save the people from their sins. How He will do it, I do not know; but He is leaving us now to begin that work.

"Is He a prophet?"

She nodded and said, "He is a prophet."

I never forgot that.

Then Jeshua came home. We had news of His work in nearby towns—how He healed the sick, and was teaching a new kingdom, a different kingdom than one we knew. We hardly had expected Him back so soon, but we were glad to see Him. Many friends called, and a feast was had in His honor. The Rabbi invited Him to read on the Sabbath. So we went—Father, Jeshua, I, Joses, Simon, and Judas—sitting on the little cushions on the men's side of the synagogue. Then the Rabbi invited Jeshua up to read. He asked the Rabbi for the roll from Esaias, and when it was procured, He opened it and then He read. I can still remember the words:

"The Spirit of the Lord God is upon me, because the Lord hath anointed Me to preach good tidings unto the meek; he hath sent Me to bind up the brokenhearted, to proclaim liberty to the captives, and the opening of the prison to them that are bound; To proclaim the acceptable year of the Lord, . . ." (Isaiah 61:1, 2) Here He stopped. There was something in His manner which held everybody in close attention. My father was leaning forward slightly, hardly breathing.

Then, "This day this scripture is fulfilled in your hearing." (See Luke 4:16-30)

There was an indrawn gasp of the assembled people. I turned to Father.

"What is He saying?"

My father turned and whispered to me, "Don't forget this, for this is true. He is saying that He is the person of whom Esaias was speaking."

"Is He the Messiah?"

"He is the Messiah."

There were accusations; and someone shouted, "Blasphemy!"

Another yelled, "If you are that prophet, let us see you do the works they say you do in Capernaum. You look to me like Jeshua, the son of old Joseph there."

Jeshua replied, "No prophet is accepted in his own country."

The whole audience seemed to be pulled by an intense anger. They arose to take Him, shouting that they would throw Him over a cliff nearby; but He stepped down and walked to the door and out, they appearing not to see Him.

My father smiled, "He will come to no harm. He has His work to do."

There is no need of my telling you all that He taught or all that He did. These things have been written, and well written, by my friends and associates.

I regret only one thing. One of our later associates, Dr. Luke, wrote an account of His life to the Greek people. I wish that He had not translated the name of my brother into that language. Proper names need not be translated, but the Doctor did it. Sometimes when I hear people now speak of Jesus Christ, I have to stop and catch myself before I realize that they are talking about my elder brother, Jeshua, the Anointed One.

The writings tell well enough of the accusations, the death—and of His resurrection. It was not until after that—when the excited Mary had told Peter and John, and they had seen the empty tomb—that we began to have clear in our minds what He meant when He so often had said He would rise the third day.

Sometime after this we were sitting on the roof of our old house in Nazareth. Peter and the apostles had organized the Church. I was appointed to be president of the Nazareth Branch. As the stars shone that night on us with all the glory of their clear beauty, I felt impelled to ask,

"Mother, was Jeshua the Son of God?"

"Yes, my son."

"But Joseph was His father."

"No, Joseph was not His father. Joseph was your father, but not His father."

"Then who was His father?"

"I have told you. He was the Son of God."

She continued:

"Years ago I was visited by an angel who told me that I should bear a son who would be called Jeshua, the Anointed One, the Son of God. Your father had intended to break the engagement when he discovered that I was expecting a baby. The angel commanded him to marry me and raise the child. These things, my sons, we have carried in our hearts all through the years: The joy of rearing, the pride of His accomplishments, the puzzlement in our souls, when He did what we least expected and when he taught new doctrine. Yet we waited, knowing God's will would be done: The agony of frustration at His death and the sight of His glorious resurrection have at least each one been put in its proper place. Remember always, my sons and daughters, He is the Son of God, literally and finally. Your mother gave Him His earthly tabernacle. Your father was privileged to act as His foster father."

I can see my mother now as she sat there in the dignity of her old age, silver-haired as she bore witness that their Jeshua, Jesus Christ to the Greeks, was the Son of God, the Redeemer. As Esaias said, " . . . Wonderful, Counsellor, The Mighty God, The everlasting Father, The Prince of Peace." (Isaiah 9:6)

She said to us, "Let us never forget it."

* * * * * * * * * *

Well, let you and me never forget it, either. He is the Son of God. He is the Prince of Peace. He is your Saviour; He is my Saviour. He was resurrected; He did establish this Church. Let us all be united in that testimony, in His holy name, Amen.

President S. Dilworth Young
Deseret Sunday School Union Conference
April 6, 1961

A Divine Birth for an Infinite Atonement

While it is true the major theme of the scriptures and the living prophets is the reality of Christ, even Jehovah, the firstborn in the spirit world, taking upon himself a tabernacle in the flesh as the literal offspring of God our Heavenly Father to redeem all mankind, that theme is inextricably tied into and finds full meaning in the parallel theme that it was his miraculous conception and birth that enabled him to perform this great mission. The divine birth must precede the divine redemption.

Unless the Savior had a God for a father, he would not have been endowed with the ability to live a sinless life, nor could he have assumed upon his shoulders the sins of the world, nor could he have broken the bands of death to enable all mankind to be resurrected. Had the Savior not had a mortal woman for a mother, he, Christ, would not have been tempted in all things, and thus would not be able to succor us in all things. In addition, having a mortal mother, Jesus inherited the seeds of physical death, enabling him to give up his life to effect his infinite atonement.

In spite of the enormous evidence that Jesus is the Son of God and that his being the Son of God is what breathes the redemptive power into the Gospel of Christ, the tragedy of the history of mankind who has embraced Christianity is a rejection of that great message either in the form of rejecting those ordinances and principles that are the lifeblood of the gospel, or in an outright rejection of Christ as the Son of God, or in a rejection of both.

"Who Knows But What Another Man Will Come Along ..."

While directing institutes of religion on different college campuses in the West, I have had several experiences that have enabled me to feel the pulse of many different people who represent a broad spectrum of commitments to so-called Christianity. Many people outside the Church—people who live lives of honor and service—evidence a solid belief in Christ's divinity. However, I have been greatly disappointed at the number of individuals in ecclesiastical positions in the Christian world who evidence an outward acceptance of Christ as the Son of God, but who in reality do not believe in his divinity. Invariably, these individuals do not openly voice rejection of Christ's divinity, but when challenged by students or others who sincerely want to know where their leaders stand on the most crucial issues in Christianity, they declare emphatically that the Savior is not divine and reject in a large measure the godly powers of the gospel.

One such experience occurred while I was directing an Institute of Religion adjacent to Colorado State University. Each year the University Religious Directors Association, of which I was a member, sponsored (with the support and encouragement of the University) a "Religious Emphasis Week." A prominent personality, one who had made significant contributions in the area of religion, would be invited to campus. During his stay, he would give several formal addresses as well as meet with smaller groups of students in the dorms and other places for informal discussion. This particular year, the invited guest was a very prominent minister of a large Protestant denomination who had served as a missionary to China for many years and was also heavily involved in civic and political activities.

Eager to support the week-long activity, I attended almost all of his formal lectures. I was very impressed with his understanding of both the Old and New Testaments. He showed excellent insight into how the doctrine and experiences of the scriptures could help us resolve the difficult national and international problems that confronted our nation. As I listened to him speak, I felt respect for this good man. He spoke often and reverently about the Lord. Indeed, I admired the sensitive qualities and teachings of our invited lecturer.

To encourage academic excellence, most universities are desirous that both the pros and cons of issues be thoroughly discussed. It was in this spirit that the university arranged for an "I disagree" session to be held at the conclusion of Religious Emphasis Week. Everyone was invited to the session, and it was arranged and advertised in such a way that it encouraged a free, open atmosphere where individuals would be willing to say what they really thought and felt. An integral part of the structure of the "I disagree" session was a panel to defend Christianity. The panel was composed of our distinguished guest, some university officials, and representatives of the major churches on campus, including myself.

After our guest's last formal sermon, those on the panel and all others who were interested filed out of the large ballroom area and down into a sizable basement room known as "the cave." Among the large number of people hurrying into the room, I noticed many who were heavily bearded, barefoot, and had forgotten to button up their shirts—representative in general of the hippie movement which was well under way at the time. As I witnessed such a sizable percentage of the "far left"—that is, those who were rebelling vigorously against society—and as I observed the loud talk and spirit of resistance to the things that had been taught all week long, it seemed the battle lines were indeed drawn, the muskets were being loaded and the swords sharpened. I thought to myself, "There is going to be an exciting time in town tonight!"

After preliminary introductions, questions and comments were invited from the audience. The response was quick in coming and in general extremely critical. One individual said he was sick and tired of Christianity because more blood had been shed under the flag of Christianity than under any other banner. Others were incensed with those who teach that there exist absolute truths, particularly in the area of sexual morality. There was a heavy emphasis on what is known as "situational ethics": the idea that one's ethics should be determined by the particular situation one might find himself in. Much was said about the "social gospel," which suggests that churches should be more involved in social action than they are. The historicity of the Old Testament prophets was strongly challenged, many saying that men like Abraham and Moses never really lived and that the stories about them in the scriptures are mythical, fabricated simply to teach moral principles. The divinity of Christ was particularly challenged: Christ, many felt, was a great teacher, but not divine—not the literal Son of God.

The thing that really shocked me was that those members of the panel who were representing Christianity were not only in agreement with most of what was being said, but were making equally strong statements repudiating the authenticity of the Bible, the concept of absolute truth, particularly in the area of morality, and especially the divine birth of Christ.

One of the most verbal ministers was a very likable individual with whom I had had a most interesting conversation just weeks before. We were leaving a meeting together and chatting about our experiences with our respective church groups on campus. I called him by name and said, "We are really having some exciting discussions in Institute on the theory of evolution." I asked him, "How do you handle the theory of evolution with your young people?"

He smiled and replied, "Oh, George, evolution is no problem because the first ten chapters of Genesis are sheer myth."

Now he and others were making similar comments, seemingly more anxious to display their scholarly training than to defend the historical authenticity of the scriptures, the absolute standards of truth contained therein, and the divinity of Christ.

While all of this was happening, I was so amazed and perturbed at what was being said that my heart was pounding uncontrollably. I'm sure I was operating on the maxim, "a closed mouth gathers no foot!" I was hesitant to stand up and say anything for fear my anxiety would keep me from making any sense. Finally, however, with some excitement, I jumped up and both microphones were quickly thrust into my hands.

I initially felt some fear, but in a few moments the fear left and an assurance came as to how important it was to bear testimony of Christ and to defend the basic tenets of Christianity. I had to infer that most of the criticism leveled that evening at Christianity was criticism of an apostate form of Christianity. I testified with all of my heart that I knew there was a God in heaven, that Jesus Christ was the literal Son of God, the Savior and Redeemer of the world. I emphasized that there were absolute truths and that each one of us would one day be held accountable for the conduct of our lives as measured by the truths of the gospel.

The audience was quiet—there was no heckling or laughing or talking—they seemed responsive and listened intently. I felt a marvelous power; in fact, I was coming on so strong in what I was saying that I could almost smell an "Abinidi" kind of smoke coming up through the floor!

I concluded by again bearing testimony of the divine Sonship of Christ and our responsibility to live by his absolute standards. When I said "Amen," much to my surprise, a spontaneous burst of applause ensued, lasting for some time. My initial reaction was "Wait a minute, why are you applauding? Most of you seemed so willing to debunk Christianity." Then it dawned on me that they were saying by their applause, "Thank God somebody knows he lives! Thank God somebody knows without question that Jesus Christ is divine, the Son of the living God. Thank God someone knows there are absolute truths!"

Just minutes after my comments, a student stood up and,

pointing to our distinguished guest, asked quite bluntly: "Sir, do you believe Jesus Christ is divine—the Son of God?" A hush came over the entire audience. Everyone looked toward the guest. He paused for several moments and then, almost with a full smile, he said: *"I would rather not believe Jesus Christ is divine, for if I did, that would give him a head start over me!"* He continued, *"Who knows but what in the next twenty years another man will come along who will live a better life than Christ, and I will revere him as my Redeemer!"*

I was stunned. Most of the people in the audience were stunned. We had listened for a week to a man who quoted the Master constantly, who claimed great respect for the Savior's teachings, who gave the distinct impression that he accepted Christ as the Son of God; but now, challenged as to where he actually stood, he unhesitatingly denied Christ's divinity. Having denied Christ's divinity the speaker negated most of what he had taught during the week.

I came away from the experience determined to do all in my power to testify clearly of the reality and importance of the Savior's divinity.

Denying the More Parts of this Gospel

There is an unmistakable, clear profile of apostasy written time and time again across the pages of Holy Writ. The pattern found in Fourth Nephi is not atypical. Two hundred years after the visit of the glorified, resurrected Christ, the Saints became lifted up in the pride of their hearts and manifested that pride by the wearing of costly apparel. They then refused to have all things in common— that is, they refused to have the welfare of every individual at heart. They next divided into classes and built up churches unto themselves, and finally they began to *"deny the more parts of his gospel,"* and they actually created a church which denied the Christ. (Fourth Nephi 29. Emphasis added)

The final manifestation of apostasy is a total rejection of the Savior as the Son of God. However, before that happens, there is a tendency for members of Christ's church to be filled with pride from academic achievements and temporal prosperity and to get caught up in the wisdom of men, giving men's precepts more credence than the revelations of God.

President J. Reuben Clark, Jr., in reiterating the fundamentals that underlie our church educational system (which, of course, are the same fundamentals that underlie the gospel itself), said that "something that may not be overlooked, forgotten, shaded, or discarded is the fact that Jesus Christ is the Son of God, the Only Begotten of the Father in the flesh." (J. Reuben Clark, Jr., address to Brigham Young University faculty, August 8, 1938.)

President Clark seemed anxious to remind us that apparently it isn't too difficult even in the Church to take away from the significance and importance of the great truth that Jesus Christ is literally the Son of God. In a day and age when so many of the traditional doctrines and values of Christianity have been changed or rejected, we can readily acknowledge that the majority of Christendom has lost much of the significant meaning found in the acceptance of the literal Sonship of Christ. But, how could rank and file LDS professional teachers, auxiliary teachers, and lay members of the Church find themselves in a similar situation?

Let me suggest that there are several ways that the importance of the divine Sonship of Christ could be weakened in the lives of members of the Church. First, it has been my observation that there is a great disparity in what is taught by and among members of the Church about the nature of fallen man and what the scriptures and the presidents of the Church seem to teach about that important subject. Secondly, I have found that either intentionally or unintentionally, many teachers have substituted the doctrine of Christ, the first principles, with the moral and ethical teachings of the gospel.

The Nature of Fallen Man

Few questions in and out of the Church elicit more excited discussion than the nature of man. In the theology of the Church, there is no question that Adam and Eve lived, that they partook of the forbidden fruit and besides physical death, brought spiritual death upon all mankind. The Church and the prophets confirm, powerfully, the fact that we all suffer from spiritual death; but, what that actually means seems to be up for grabs by many Church members.

Perhaps one of the best elaborations as to what the scriptures mean when they speak of man's fallen nature is the following by the late Sidney B. Sperry, a former colleague of mine and former dean of the College of Religious Instruction at Brigham Young University.

> All men, whether "incorrigible sinners" or so-called "good men" who are ethical and just, "the honorable men of the earth," (D&C 76:75) are carnal and fallen as long as they fail to become "new creatures" by yielding to "the enticings of the Holy Spirit" and by laying aside the "natural man" and becoming saints through the atonement of our Lord (Mosiah 3:19). In other words, men must be spiritually reborn, even as the Lord taught Nicodemus, or they cannot see the kingdom of God (John 3:3). Now we suppose that Nicodemus was an ethical, just, and honorable man in his relationships to others; nevertheless, the Savior made it perfectly clear that he had to have a spiritual rebirth or he would remain, as Book of Mormon language has it, a "fallen" or "natural" man.
>
> When the Nephite record refers to fallen man as "carnal, sensual, and devilish," it seems to shock some people—and it should. But let us here introduce the following explanation by Dr. David Yarn of Brigham Young University:

An explanation ... suggests ... that the words *carnal, sensual,* and *devilish,* must not be limited to their more narrow and specific connotations, but that they are accurately, though more broadly, interpreted by the scriptural phrase "enemy to God." That is to say, not all men who have not made covenants with the Christ are given to indulging in practices which are appropriately designated carnal, sensual, and devilish in a dictionary sense. Yet, all men, regardless of how moral and how pure they may be with reference to such practices, are enemies to God, until they yield to the enticings of the Holy Spirit, accept the Atonement of the Lord, and are submissive to His will. A significant point here is that what we conventionally call basic personal and social morality is not enough ... for one not to be an enemy to God he must endeavor to do all things whatsoever the Lord his God shall command him (See Abraham 3:25).

Summarily put, the natural man (he who is carnal, sensual and devilish, he who is an enemy to God) is the man who has not humbled himself before God and made covenants with God by receiving the revealed ordinances at the hands of God's authorized servants; or the man who, having done all these things, has failed to live according to the covenants made in baptism and to the injunction given when he was confirmed a member of the Church—"Receive the Holy Ghost." (Gospel Living in the Home, p. 51, Deseret Sunday School Union, 1962)

(Sidney B. Sperry, *The Problems of the Book of Mormon*, Salt Lake City: Bookcraft, 1964, pp. 5-6.)

It is important, when the nature of fallen man is discussed, to emphasize that because of the atonement of Christ we are not born with original guilt—we are not born in a depraved condition. We are born pure, holy, and innocent, and by virtue of the atonement we are born with the light of Christ enabling us to know good from evil as easily as we know night from day. Consequently, all mankind is born free! We, at birth, are redeemed from the Fall.

However, in spite of our being born free, of our having the light of Christ, when we reach the age of accountability we all (except Christ) suffer from spiritual death; we are all sinners (Romans 3:23); we are, as Adam was told, "conceived in sin, even so when they [children] begin to grow up, sin conceiveth in their hearts, and they taste the bitter that they may know to prize the good." (Moses 6:55.)

In addition, it is important for us to realize that there is a difference in the nature of fallen man and the potential of fallen man. Because all of us suffer from spiritual death doesn't mean we do not have marvelous potential. In fact, the declaration "We are born to be Gods" confirms that our potential is as great as is God's.

When the prophets speak of the nature of "natural man," they are describing those attitudes and actions that are "natural" as a result of having become fallen. As an example, when it comes to mankind as a whole, is it "natural" for them, of themselves, to know God and Christ? Is it "natural" for them to respond to or accept the message of the Restoration? Is it "natural" for most people to take care of the poor? Is it "natural" for mankind in general to live in peace?

And how about members of the Church: is it "natural" for most members to pay an honest tithe, give generous fast offerings, marry in the temple, do their home teaching and visiting teaching? Statistics indicate and personal experience confirms that it takes a tremendous effort on the part of the Lord, his Holy Spirit, his anointed prophets, and those who labor in the Church to get a small percentage of people inclined toward the fulness of the gospel and to get the membership of the Church to come alive in the powers of heaven.

I believe with all of my heart that *if* we become truly converted to the restored gospel of Christ (and only *if!*), we *can* arrive at a point where it will be "natural" for us to pay an honest tithe and a generous fast offering, to marry in the temple and give our energy, time and talents to build the kingdom of God. However, I'm fully convinced that if it were not for the restoration of the gospel, for the holy priesthood, for the gift and power of the Holy Ghost, for the inspired pleading of living prophets in our midst; if it were not for a decided effort on our part to humble ourselves, to hunger and thirst and strive and seek for righteousness, we would forever remain subject to the flesh, taking our cues constantly from the flesh (the mind) instead of from the Spirit. We would forever be spiritually dead, incapable of comprehending our God-like potential, and we would remain candidates of the terrestrial or telestial kingdom.

Personally, I'm quite overwhelmed at what a challenge it is to subdue the flesh and to yield to the spirit. I'm both fascinated and appalled at how hard it is to keep hold of the iron rod, to really keep the mind and heart right where they should be. I have a personal testimony of the necessity of clinging to the iron rod (1 Nephi 8:24). It isn't terribly difficult to be basically good, but how hard it is to pull down the revelations of heaven, to be filled with the love of God and obtain the power to make a difference in the lives of others. I can appreciate why President David O. McKay said:

> Man has a dual nature; one, related to the earthly or animal life, the other akin to the divine. Whether man remains satisfied within what we designate the animal world, satisfied with what the animal world will give him, yielding without effort to the whim of his appetites

and passions and slipping farther and farther into the realm of indulgence, or whether through self-mastery, he rises toward intellectual, moral and spiritual enjoyments depends upon the kind of choice he makes every day, every hour of his life." (*Gospel Ideals*, pp. 347-348.)

The achievement of the self-mastery President McKay speaks of is only by and through the gospel for he declared, "The whole purpose of life is to bring under subjection the animal passions, proclivities, and tendencies that we might realize the companionship of God's Holy Spirit." (*Improvement Era*, May 1964, p. 349.) On another occasion President McKay said further:

> Only in the complete surrender of our inner life may we rise above the sordid, selfish pull of nature ... there is none other name under heaven given among men, whereby we must be saved ... I like to associate with the word saved the power that man gets in this life to rise above his animal instincts and passions, power to overcome or resist social evils that blight men's and women's souls and shut them out, not only from the peace of the world, but also from citizenship in the Kingdom of God. Men may yearn for peace, cry for peace, and work for peace, but there will be no peace until they follow the path pointed out by the living Christ. (*Improvement Era*, October 1960, p. 703.)

This question of the nature of fallen man is crucial in our search to know Christ, because if we as Latter-day Saints reject the seriousness of man's fallen condition and teach that natural man is basically good instead of the correct concept that man has a dual nature, then we take away from the awesome necessity and importance of Christ being the Son of God, for Christ was sired by God that he might obtain the power to free mankind to become, if they will, as he is; to reach a condition where it is natural to abhor sin, natural to keep the commandments, and natural to love all mankind with a perfect love. When we sense deeply by the revelations of heaven the total and complete incapability of mankind to bring about his own deliverance from sin, ignorance and death; when we observe by reasoning alone that mankind unaided by God cannot solve the most basic temporal and economic problems; when we become mindful that the overall history of mankind has been one where war has been much more predominant than peace, where selfishness is much more common than generosity, then we will see the absolute need of a divine Redeemer and we will do all in our power to avail ourselves of the mighty atonement of Christ. I'm convinced that there isn't anything in the gospel of Christ that will cause us to be more determined and more effective in obtaining the power of Godliness than to glimpse by revelation the seriousness of our own fallen condition. On the other hand, there isn't anything more in my estimation, that keeps the Saints from enjoying the power they could have than getting caught up in the wisdom of men, the materialism of our day, and a sense of self-confidence that in their own abilities they can fulfill their missions on earth. To help us understand how totally dependent we are on the Savior and how impossible it is to free ourselves from our condition, consider the following analogy.

The man of whom we speak in this analogy is representative of those who see themselves as quite bright, well educated, emotionally stable, doing well in a chosen vocation or profession and in general feel they have prospered according to their own genius. (Alma 30:17).

Our friend is challenged by an associate to run a thirty mile marathon which, if he does successfully between sunrise and sunset, will receive many prestigious honors. However, this is no ordinary marathon for it covers an area where there are many different types of terrain—some gently rolling, some quite steep, (including a sizable mountain) plus an area dotted by swampland. Although he is mindful that it will be a tremendous challenge, our friend doesn't know that it is virtually impossible for any human being to successfully cover the distance prescribed within a day—he has accepted the challenge on good faith that it can be done. His situation is somewhat akin to Adam and Eve's predicament in the Garden of Eden where they were given the dual commandments to multiply and replenish the earth and were forbidden to partake of the tree of knowledge of good and evil— two commandments which simply could not be kept simultaneously.

Having great confidence in his own ability plus enjoying a lot of spunk and determination (two ingredients that are good in and of themselves and so necessary to survive the challenges of mortality) he accepts the challenge and the following morning is ready at the crack of dawn for his great adventure.

As the sun slips up over the eastern horizon, the starting gun is fired and he is on his way. His optimism is high as he runs swiftly over the gently rolling landscape—he's convinced, in fact, because of the miles he covers in the first hour, that it will be quite easy to achieve his goal. However, the terrain steepens and his pace slackens. As he climbs higher on the mountain itself he is no longer running but struggles in a slow, laborious way to negotiate the steep cliffs.

Eventually, after great effort, he reaches the summit and commences his descent down into the valley but he is deeply disturbed because it took him much longer to get to the summit than he hoped it would. He makes good time, however, going down the mountain, and again feels confident that he can still reach his goal. However, as he enters the valley he is troubled because he must now work his way across a sizable area of swampland. He glances toward the sky and is disappointed that the sun has crossed well past the mid-point of its journey. Now, more than ever, he must take great care to stay on solid ground and not step into areas where there very well could be treacherous quicksand.

After spending some time carefully crossing the swamp, he again checks the position of the sun and is startled to realize he has only a few hours at most to reach his goal. Having initially been very careful crossing the swamp, he becomes a little careless, even reckless as he hurries faster and faster. Almost before he realizes what he has done, he finds himself walking on ground that appeared safe but is now quivering under his feet—he frantically reverses his direction to seek more stable footing but the ground gives way and he is caught in quicksand.

Although he realizes his predicament is quite serious and he is somewhat angry to have used poor judgment in allowing himself to be trapped, because he has always been a man of great confidence and self assurance, he is totally convinced he can remove himself from his predicament on the basis of his own power. He calmly attempts to move his feet forward but to no avail. He then vigorously attempts to thrash his legs but the faster and harder he tries to extricate himself the quicker he sinks deeper into the quicksand. Sensing for the first time the awful seriousness of his predicament, in a fit of total irrationality he reaches down into the quicksand, takes hold of his boot straps and proceeds to pull and pull for all he's worth! He then realizes how foolish it is to try to free himself by pulling on his own bootstraps! His embarrassment is heightened as he remembers his extensive academic training and his remarkable ability in times past to be calm and controlled at all times.

Finally, our friend admits that on the basis of his own ability he simply cannot free himself. He knows he must have help from some other source and the help must be found quickly. For the first time he becomes aware that just inches ahead, a strong branch of a tree is within reach. (In our analogy the branch and tree represent the combined wisdom and strength of mankind.) With tremendous effort our friend inches forward and finally grasps the thick branch with both hands. Oh, what a relief it is to him, what an assurance to have hold of something that seems so solid and so sure! After resting for a few moments, he begins to pull himself up on the branch—it takes a great deal of effort, but the more he successfully pulls his body onto the branch, the more confidence he has that surely the branch will be the means of his salvation from the quicksand. In fact, even before he has managed to lift himself out of the muck and mire of the quicksand there return his familiar feelings of independence and self-confidence, even a pride that is akin to arrogance. Finally, with one great lurch, he pulls himself completely onto the limb—but as he does, he hears a terrifying crack and the limb snaps off, plunging him back into the quicksand. Having expended so much energy and effort, having placed so much confidence in what he was sure was his sole source of redemption, our friend is intellectually, emotionally and physically wiped out—he continues to struggle, but he now knows in a way he has never known before that his predicament is totally and completely hopeless. There is no way on the basis of his own strength or the strength of the combined wisdom of men that he can be freed from imminent death.

As he sinks deeper into the quicksand the panorama of his entire life passes before him. Things which had once seemed so important now seem so puerile or childish. His lifelong ambition to be acknowledged as unusually bright and the most successful in his profession, to own the finest home and the most expensive car—all of these ambitions fade into utter insignificance. He begins to realize that his relationships with others, especially with his family, are of utmost and supreme importance. He is utterly desolated with the clear realization that he has allowed his appetites to be abused and debauched by relentless unethical advertizing campaigns that artificially stimulate men's appetites. He begins to sense the eternal verity of God and Christ and the hereafter. He is very uneasy about the prospect of death, for he is only now appreciating the significance of life and oh, how he wants to live! The hills in the distance, the trees, the sky, the sun—all things seem to take on a greater beauty and significance. During what appear to be the final moments of his life there arises from deep within his changed heart an indiscribable confidence that somehow there is a divine purpose in life; that through the intervention of a higher supreme power he can find deliverance from death.

The sand has covered his shoulders and is gradually oozing up his neck. He is reaching, still reaching upward, hoping against hope that somehow, something will happen. His face is turned upward that he might breathe as long as possible, when much to his astonishment, there appear an arm and a hand extending toward him—an arm and a hand actually within reach!

He recognizes immediately that the arm and hand are powerful. Because of his predicament, our friend doesn't rationalize for a moment. He doesn't intellectualize how an arm and a hand can be hanging in mid-air! He simply realizes that if there is any hope for redemption it will be in that hand and arm. He reaches upward and clasps the extended hand. As soon as he does he feels a kind of power like he's never felt before. He feels a power coming into his hand and whole being that generates a confidence, a trust, a faith, a perfect assurance that in this new power he can and will be freed from his predicament. He hangs on with all the strength and determination he can muster. He feels himself being lifted out of the mire—oh, what a struggle! Having waited so long to acknowledge his incapabilities, having waited because of a proud heart, he now knows that the process and experience of becoming freed will not only require a supernatural power, but it will require all the courage and strength *he* can rally to hold on to the extended hand.

As he struggles to hold on he feels his hand slipping, not because of a lack of power in the other hand, but because of a lack of strength in his own. Try as hard as he can, he isn't able to hold on, his hand slips out, and he falls back into the quicksand. But (and this is the great message of the Gospel of Jesus Christ), our friend quickly looks up to where the hand was and the hand is still there! He quickly takes hold again. The struggle again ensues, and in time, using all the persistence, determination, strength and faith he can muster, he is able to avail himself fully of the means of redemption that is afforded him. Ultimately, he is raised out of the quicksand that almost became his tomb, and placed on solid rock.

He soon realizes that he was not only delivered from the awful possibility of death but he is a different person. He is clean from the effects of swamp water, mud and sand. As the full realization of his deliverance and the tremendous change that has come over him sinks into his heart, he falls upon his knees and with profound expressions of gratitude he acknowledges that it was a power greater than any and all other powers on earth that enabled him to be delivered—oh, the expression of joy; the ecstasy that fills his being as he contemplates the loving kindness and tender goodness of his God and his Redeemer! The psalmist wrote, "He brought me up also out of an horrible pit, out of mire clay and set my feet upon a rock, and established my goings." (Psalms 40:2).

We are, then, totally dependent upon the Lord to be reclaimed from our fallen condition. All the combined wisdom and learning of man cannot change our nature and free us from our predicament. Rather than simply stressing self-sufficiency, our emphasis should be self-sufficiency in Christ. We need to reach with all the energy we possess to make contact with the Lord, but it is his power that changes our lives.

Another way people deliberately or otherwise take away from the central truth that Jesus Christ is the Son of God is by confusing what the gospel is and what it is not. Strictly speaking, the gospel is the "glad tidings" or "good news" that the Son of God, tabernacled in the flesh, suffered, died, and rose again to "sanctify the world and to cleanse it from all unrighteousness." (D&C 76:41.)

I genuinely fear that there are many among us who emphasize, in the name of the Gospel of Jesus Christ, little more than the moral and ethical teachings of the gospel. In fact, it very well could be true that if one were to remove the moral and ethical teachings and the psychological, sociological and philosophical truths from the theology of many Saints, nothing would be left. I'm somewhat troubled when I often find it difficult to locate many of the golden strands of the restored gospel in the fabric of what is said and written by well meaning Saints. I'm also troubled when I come away from sermons heard or books read with the distinct impression that somehow if it weren't for the new-found psychological and sociological insights and the clever techniques to apply them, there would be no hope, no possibility of people ever overcoming their weaknesses and idiosyncrasies. I believe those tendencies take away from a dynamic faith in Jesus Christ, a faith that would suggest that in him and him alone can we find the strength and power and capacity to become totally like him.

This problem reminds me of an article written in the ward newspaper of a student ward at a prominent university. The article was entitled, "What's Happened to the Scriptures?" The gist of the article was that there must be a new set of standard works in the Church, for observation had shown that current popular writers like Kahlil Gibran, Eric Fromme, and others were quoted much, much more than Moses or Paul or Peter or Moroni or Joseph Smith or the current prophet. While obviously there is wisdom in the writings of good men outside the Church, it seems ironic that sometimes Latter-day Saints are more interested in quoting popular, clever writers than the Lord's prophets.

President J. Reuben Clark, in the same address referred to earlier, said, "Students fully sense the hollowness of teachings which would make the gospel plan a mere system of ethics, they know that Christ's teachings are in the highest degree ethical, but they also know they are more than this." It is important to realize that the moral and ethical teachings that are found in Christ's gospel are contained in every major religion of mankind; even a cursory study of Buddhism, Mohammedanism, or Zoroastrianism, reveals powerful commitments to such ideals as love, kindness, patience, integrity, respect for life, etc. It is important also to realize that an understanding of the moral and ethical teachings and an effort to live them will bless all who do so but never, worlds without end, will such an approach by itself change the fallen nature of man and prepare a person for exaltation in the kingdom of God.

The famous author William Blake saw clearly how unfortunate it is that so many Christians see Christianity as simply a system of ethics:

> What can this Gospel of Jesus be?
> What life and immortality,
> What was it that he brought to light
> That Plato and Cicero did not write?
> The heathen dieties wrote them all,
> The moral virtues great and small

The power of redemption centers in and is obtained from the great atonement. Growing out of the atonement are peculiar principles and ordinances that of themselves have no redemptive power but are so constructed as to stimulate faith and be a channel for the power of Christ to flow into our lives. As we receive from Christ his power through the ordinances and principles, as we are transformed in his image and we become like him, we are moral and ethical in all we do, but we are much, much more than that; for in addition, we know Christ, we understand the reality of his redemption, and we enjoy a character and a love that are immeasureably greater than the character and love that are available outside the fulness of the gospel.

If we keep this distinction in mind, we will always recognize Christ as the source of power and everything else in the gospel as a means to obtain that power. If we see the Savior as the source of redemptive power, I believe we will stress the necessity of a dynamic faith in him and the importance of the Holy Ghost to change our lives instead of vesting sizable portions of our time, energy and money in intricate systems of behavioral change that are as bereft of godly power to change human nature as are the theologies of apostate Christianity.

President John Taylor pinpointed the problem we are discussing. He clearly saw and declared in power that the Savior came not to renew or emphasize a system of ethics, but rather to bring a way of life that includes all that is ethical but goes infinitely beyond a mere system of ethics. Speaking of man's innate limitations, President Taylor said:

> As a man, through the power of his body, he could attain to the dignity and completeness of manhood, but could go no further; as a man, he is born, as a man, he lives, and as a man, he dies; but through the essence and power of the Godhead, which is in him, which descended to him as the gift of God from his Heavenly Father, he is capable of rising from the contracted limits of manhood to the dignity of God. (John Taylor, *The Mediation and Atonement*, Salt Lake City: Steven & Wallis, Inc., 1950, p. 139.)

The essence and power of man cannot lift you nor me above the limits of mankind, but the Savior can and the reason he can is because he is the Son of God.

You and I cannot enjoy the greater powers available in the restored gospel unless we sense in a profound way our total dependency upon Jesus Christ and that only in and through him can our nature be changed and our character become like his. To know that Jesus is literally the Son of God is to acknowledge that because of that divine sonship he was able to come to the earth, break the bands of sin and death, and offer through his divine gospel the power to become totally like him.

Chapter 4

To Know The Lord Is To Know By Personal Revelation The Reality Of The Savior's Atoning Sacrifice For Us

The atonement of Christ is the most important event that has transpired or ever will transpire among all of God's creations. It is the very source of all life, light, power, truth and love, and the very center and object of all redemptive faith. To have faith in Jesus Christ is to have faith in his atonement, for the entire purpose of the Savior's life was to come forth to suffer, die, and rise again: "For this is the gospel, the glad tidings which the voice out of the heavens bore record unto us—that he came into the world, even Jesus, to be crucified for the world, and to bear the sins of the world, and to sanctify the world, and to cleanse it from all unrighteousness." (D&C 76:40-41.) The prophet Joseph, after testifying of the central truth of the atonement, declared that "all other things that pertain to our religion are only appendages to it." (*TPJS* p. 121.)

In other words, the atonement is the very heart of the gospel of Jesus Christ. Even as the human heart pumps life-giving blood to all parts of the body, so will the atonement, if understood properly, act as a great spiritual heart, pumping life-giving blood through the ordinances and principles of the gospel to the life and soul of every member of the Church. Is it any wonder that every ordinance and principle, as indicated in the first chapter, is given from God to man to typify or foreshadow the Savior and his atonement? Is it any wonder that all the precious testimonies of men and women who have felt the redeeming power of the Savior in their lives have as their central theme the majesty and grandeur of that great act?

Even though the atonement occurred nearly 2,000 years ago, its reality to us and its impact on us can be as great as though we had been contemporaries with the Savior living in Jerusalem. Indeed, under the quiet workings of the Holy Ghost we can stand, as it were, in the Garden of Gethsemane, a witness of the Savior's agony; we can stand, as it were, at the foot of Golgotha and obtain an overwhelming awareness of the pain of the cross; we can have come into our hearts, at least in a measure and only as the Spirit can reveal it, the tremendous pain, sorrow, and humiliation he suffered. We can, in other words, experience, in part, the majesty of the atonement and make it the single greatest event in our lives.

The following experience of Orson F. Whitney's shows how real the atonement can become in one's life:

> It was in a dream, or in a vision in a dream, as I lay upon my bed in the little town of Columbia, Lancaster County, Pennsylvania [while on a mission]. I seemed to be in the Garden of Gethsemane, a witness of the Savior's agony. I saw Him as plainly as I have seen anyone. Standing behind a tree in the foreground, I beheld Jesus with Peter, James and John, as they came through a little wicket gate at my right. Leaving the three Apostles there, after telling them to kneel and pray, the Son of God passed over to the other side, where He also

knelt and prayed. It was the same prayer with which all Bible readers are familiar: "Oh, my Father, if it be possible, let this cup pass from me; nevertheless, not as I will but as Thou wilt."

As He prayed, the tears streamed down His face, which was toward me. I was so moved at the sight that I also wept, out of pure sympathy. My whole heart went out to Him; I loved Him with all my soul, and longed to be with Him as I longed for nothing else.

Presently, He arose and walked to where those Apostles were kneeling—fast asleep! He shook them gently, awoke them, and in a tone of tender reproach, untinctured by the least show of anger or impatience, asked them plaintively if they could not watch with Him one hour. There He was, with the awful weight of the world's sins upon His shoulders, with the pangs of every man, woman and child shooting through His sensitive soul—and they would not watch with Him one poor hour!

Returning to His place, He offered up the same prayer as before; then went back and again found them sleeping. Again he awoke them, readmonished them, and once more returned and prayed. Three times this occurred, until I was perfectly familiar with His appearance—face, form and movements. He was of noble stature and majestic mien—not at all the weak, effeminate being that some painters have portrayed; but the very God that He was and is, as meek and humble as a little child.

All at once the circumstance seemed to change, the scene remaining just the same. Instead of before, it was after the crucifixion, and the Savior, with the three Apostles, now stood together in a group at my left. They were about to depart and ascend to Heaven. I could endure it no longer. I ran from behind the tree, fell at his feet, clasped Him around the knees, and begged Him to take me with Him.

I shall never forget the kind and gentle manner in which he stooped, raised me up and embraced me. It was so vivid, so real. I felt the very warmth of His body, as He held me in His arms and said in tenderest tones: "No my son; these have finished their work; they can go with me; but you must stay and finish yours." Still I clung to Him. Gazing up into His face—for He was taller than I—I besought Him fervently: "Well, promise me that I will come to you at the last." Smiling sweetly, He said, "That will depend entirely upon yourself!" I awoke with a sob in my throat, and it was morning." (Quoted in Bryant S. Hinckley, *Faith of Our Pioneer Fathers*, pp. 211-212.)

President Harold B. Lee once alluded to a similar experience of his:

As one of the humblest among you, and occupying the station I do, I want to bear you my humble testimony that I have received by the voice and the power of revelation, the knowledge and an understanding that God is.

It was a week following the conference, when I was preparing myself for a radio talk on the life of the Savior, when I read again the story of the life, the crucifixion and the resurrection of the Master—there came to me as I read that, a reality of that story, more than just what was on the written page. For in truth, *I found myself viewing the scenes with a certainty as though I had been there in person*. I know that these things come by the revelations of the living God. ("Divine Revelation," Speeches of the Year, BYU, October 15, 1952, p. 12. Emphasis added.)

As we are endowed with the kind of understanding that came to Orson F. Whitney and President Lee, we can offer the required sacrifice of a broken heart and a contrite spirit. The Savior in turn can offer us the promise of redemption from our personal sins, total freedom from ignorance, and the promise of a glorious resurrection. Again, I testify from my experience that one can understand the gospel fully, live life abundantly, assist others to their godly potential, and achieve the promise of eternal life only by experiencing profoundly and personally the significance and actuality of the atonement.

The Lord is aware, even as we should be, that the very course of our lives is determined not so much by what we know about a particular thing, but rather by how we feel about it. In fact, it is one of the most evident truths of existence that the degree to which we feel about something will determine the degree to which it has an impact in our lives. Therefore, the Lord is anxious that we feel more deeply and profoundly about his atonement than we feel about anything else in life. He is anxious to endow us, if we will seek for it, with an understanding of and intensity of feeling about the atonement that is so great it will motivate us to forsake our sins, keep his commandments, and honor, love and serve him forever.

The Doctrine of the Atonement

To prepare ourselves for the "feeling" dimension of the atonement, we need first to grasp intellectually the doctrine of the atonement. The beginning of our understanding will come as we strive to comprehend the seriousness of personal sin, the demands of justice and the role of mercy.

Because of the fall of Adam, circumstances on earth are such that all of us, when we become accountable (eight years of age), commit sins. The sins we commit cause us to become unclean and consequently unfit for entrance back into the presence of God. As we sin, we actually contaminate both our body and spirit. It appears that the contamination or uncleanness occurs because each time we sin, the spirit and power of the adversary is present and quite literally pulsates through our body.

Justice demands that for every broken law (sin), there is a penalty affixed, and the penality is suffering. Somehow the demands of justice are so great that if we must pay them, we will have to suffer even as Christ suffered (D&C 17:19). However, because of the atonement, the demands of justice can be fully met in our behalf by the Savior, if we repent and exercise faith in him. The beauty of having the Savior's mercy satisfy justice in our behalf, is that in the process, we not only are forgiven of our sins, but we become like the Savior. This occurs because in the process of repentance and living the gospel, we go through the Savior. We involve ourselves in his power and in his divine nature, which enables us to become like him. People who resist the fulness of the gospel, refusing to repent and accept Christ's atonement, will satisfy the demands of justice by suffering for their own sins. However, because they do not go through the Savior in the process of repentance, they do not become like him and are consequently heirs of either the telestial or terrestrial degree of glory.

Although this elaboration on the doctrine of the atonement is somewhat brief, perhaps it will provide at least a framework to use in coming to a better appreciation of the idea that the atonement is very personal. The Savior came to free individuals from sin. He assumed upon his shoulders each of our sins, not simply those of "mankind." If we view the atonement in the context of an experience that the Savior went through for us individually, it will make a great deal of difference in its impact on our personal lives.

A Personal Testimony

After completing my junior year at Brigham Young University and while yet in our first year of marriage, my wife and I left school and moved to the farm to assist my ailing father. Four days before high school started that fall, I received an appointment to teach seminary full time. My first assignment was to teach the life of Christ.

What a challenging but exciting year that first year of teaching was for me! Not having had any education classes, I sensed deeply my lack of training, and I was amazed at the amount of reading and studying each day's teaching required. I didn't have the problem of teaching over the students' heads, for I wasn't knowledgeable enough. In fact, most of what I taught each day I had learned the night before, so at least it was fresh! It was a heavy burden to farm a hundred acres, milk twenty cows, and teach seminary. Nevertheless, that year was one of the most thrilling teaching years of my life.

I appreciated the supplementary material given us as teachers, but found it extremely difficult to use lesson outlines prepared by someone else. After trying valiantly for several weeks, yet feeling a deeper and deeper sense of frustration, I finally pulled the New Testament front and center and dove into it with all the energy I could muster. Oh, the excitement that came! I could hardly wait to get into the classroom each day to share the new insights that unfolded. I sensed that the students also felt of my excitement, and they responded in the same way. Together, we followed the scriptural account of the Savior's premortal existence, his birth, youth, and ministry. As I studied the Savior's life more deeply than I ever had before, every phase of my life seemed to take on a greater meaning. It was a profound spiritual awakening for me.

By the time we had progressed into the latter part of the Savior's ministry, winter had come and gone and a new spring was upon us. I always felt such a physical rejuvenation with the coming of another spring. My spirits were always lifted, I invariably felt a kind of new beginning, and I had an overwhelming awareness of God's goodness in bringing such a newness of life to the earth once again. As the snow melted under the increased warmth of the spring sun and the buds began bursting forth in another cycle of life, I felt pleasure in plowing the moist soil amidst circling sea gulls, planting crops once again in anticipation of another harvest.

And what a glorious privilege to teach the life of Christ! I felt an inner radiance increasing from new understandings and new appreciations, and I sensed as never before the symbolism of the atonement in the unfolding of a new spring. With these feelings and the approach of the Easter season, I desired more than anything else to plant in the hearts of my precious students a special understanding of the atonement, that they might harvest a profound newness of life through the mercy, merits, and grace of Christ.

As I finished my classes the day before I was to teach the atonement of Christ, I gathered together several books of my own and some from the seminary library that I thought would be helpful—the scriptures, Talmage's *Jesus the Christ*, and several historical works about the Savior—carried them out to the car and dumped them in the back seat, drove home, changed my clothes, and went out in the fields to plow and harrow. About sundown I came in, had supper, and then went out to the barn to milk the cows. It was after ten that evening when I finished milking and came back into the house. I felt real excitement as I cleaned up a bit and carried my books in to the kitchen table.

Everything about the evening is yet vivid. Diane and a baby daughter were asleep in the bedroom. I can still see in my mind's eye the white muslin curtains at the window and even the design of the wallpaper on the kitchen walls. I laid my books out on the tiny pinewood table, and then I knelt in prayer and asked my Heavenly Father that I might understand more fully what the atonement was all about, that somehow, on the morrow, I might help my precious students understand and accept what the Savior had done for them. I then sat down and began to review the scriptural account of the concluding week of the Savior's life.

There were no open visions that night, no audible voices, but as I read and pondered the scriptures, it was as though I was there witnessing the scenes as they unfolded. For the first time in my life, I felt so deeply the sorrow and pain the Savior went through that I thought my heart would break. For the first time in my life, while reading the scriptures, I wept openly. Somehow, previous to that evening, I hadn't felt a really deep commitment on my part to the Savior, and perhaps that was because never before had I felt such a deep and profound commitment on his part to me! Before that evening, I had always viewed his suffering and sorrow in almost a detached way—almost as a spectator. I had felt, to a degree, how marvelous it was that he was the Savior of mankind, that he had suffered for everyone, but that night I was overwhelmed at the atonement he performed in my behalf, the suffering he went through for me—not only the suffering he went through for me, but the suffering he went through because of me! That evening, the reality of the Savior's atonement, his sorrow, humiliation and pain sank deeper into my heart than the reality of anything else in life. Especially this was so of Gethsemane. Again, although I saw no visions and heard no voices, it was as though I were actually there.

On that spring night in the tiny farm house, something else that brought extremely deep feelings was reading about the Roman scourging the Savior suffered. The Romans referred to their scourging as a "half-way death": if administered beyond a prescribed time, it could be fatal. Historical evidence suggests that convicted criminals were either scourged or crucified, but rarely subjected to both forms of punishment, as was Christ. The scriptural account implies that Pilate ordered Christ to be scourged, not because he felt Christ was guilty of any crime, but because he had hoped it would satisfy the Jews. Pilate hoped not to have the terrible responsibility of approving Christ's crucifixion. As I studied, I visualized in my mind's eye a typical Roman scourging, but in my heart, with the help of the Spirit, I felt deeply the awfulness of that terrible ordeal.

I could see the individual who was to be scourged led by the Roman centurions into a small courtyard, in the center of which were several stone pillars about three feet high. Steel rings were embedded on either side of the pillars, close to the ground. The clothes would be stripped from the victim's back and he would be forced to bend over, resting his chest on the top of the pillar, his hands having been securely tied in the rings. A Roman centurion would stand to the side, holding in his hand a flagellum, or whip, which was made of a short, curved piece of wood to which were attached several strips of leather. Sewn into the end of each piece of leather were jagged pieces of bone or metal.

At a given signal, the centurion would commence the scourging by bringing the flagellum in a powerful swing over his shoulder onto the exposed back of the victim. With one stroke of the whip, the flesh would be laid bare to the bone. The entire experience would last probably only minutes. That night, I sensed as never before the brutality of the scourging and the pain it brought the Savior.

I then continued to follow the scriptural account of the last moments of the Savior's life. Following the scourging, the Roman soldier placed a robe on the Savior, a plaited crown of thorns on his head, and led him out of the city to a small hill called Golgotha, or the Place of the Skull. Though the Savior undoubtedly possessed a strong body, because of his suffering in Gethsemane, his spending the entire night in abusive treatment before Annas, Caiaphas, Herod and Pilate, and because of the scourging, he did not have the strength to carry the cross upon which he would be crucified. Some historians feel that the Savior attempted to carry only the crosspiece, and not the entire cross. The uprights were often left intact between crucifixions, especially in such prominent places of crucifixion as Golgotha. If this were so, the crosspiece was probably not more than six feet long and perhaps five inches square, weighing probably around 60 or 70 pounds. However heavy it was, the Savior could not carry it, and Simon the Cyrene was pressed into service to carry the cross.

By the time the Savior arrived at the top of the small hill, his mother, several other women, and the apostle John were already there. I imagined that John the Beloved, after learning of the impending crucifixion, had hurried to the little village of Bethany to inform the Savior's mother of the fateful event. The terrible experience would be all the more difficult for the Savior, knowing his mother would be a witness to his agony; and yet it had been prophetically foretold Mary that "Yea, a spear shall pierce through him to the wounding of thy own soul." (I.V. Luke 2:35.) That wounding of Mary's soul would take place that day.

I had read many times before of how the Romans stripped the Savior of his clothes before girding him with a loin cloth, but that night I sensed deeply what the removal of his clothes must have meant in terms of embarrassment. He who would possess, as it were, an infinite sense of modesty, was subjected to such terrible indignity. That experience must have been in part the humiliation Paul the apostle spoke of (Acts 8:33). Again, I felt quite overwhelmed that the Savior would be willing to go through such humiliation for me.

The Romans had tried many different methods of putting people to death: boiling in oil, beheading, impalement with a spear, suffocation, and others. But none was so terrible, so effective as crucifixion, for that method, devised by the Phoenicians, extended the pain and suffering over a period of many days. The Romans were skilled in crucifying: when they finally subdued the slave rebellion led by Spartacus, they crucified 6,000 men in a single day.

Reading all I could find on the historical background of Roman crucifixion and then studying the accounts of that event in the New Testament, I sensed vividly the cruelty of the manner of the Savior's death. After arriving at Golgotha, the crosspiece was laid on the ground behind the Savior. Then a Roman centurion on either side would reach up, grab an arm, and pull him quickly to the ground. Spreading the palms of his hands on the crosspiece, the centurion would then drive a five to seven-inch square-ended nail through his palm. To assure that the hand would not pull free from the nail, another nail was driven through the wrist. Quickly moving to the other side, the centurion did the same to the other hand and wrist. Two centurions next took hold of the ends of the crosspiece, dragging the Savior over to the upright. Lifting the crosspiece to the top of the upright, the soldiers fit it into the precut notch and nailed it in place. Then, buckling his legs in order to put the soles of his feet flat on the upright, they drove large nails through the thick part of his feet.

Hanging in that unnatural position, the pectoral muscles along the sides of the chest soon knotted, making it almost impossible to breathe. The only way the Lord could have continued to breathe would have been to put all the weight of his body on the nails in his feet and push up, relieving the arm and chest muscles so that normal breathing could be restored. But the pain in his feet soon would have become so excessive that he would have to drop back down. The Savior, like others who were victims of the cross, would have been constantly writhing in pain.

The Jews, eager to honor their own Sabbath, demanded that Jesus and the thieves be killed and their bodies removed before the Sabbath commenced at sundown on Friday. The centurions assigned to that detail arrived at the scene having a large cudgel (stick or club) and a two or three foot, one inch thick board. Walking up to a thief on one side, a centurion held the board behind the big bone in the upper part of the leg while another centurion hit the bone and snapped it in two. The same was done to the other leg, and death would follow quickly.

After breaking the legs of both thieves, a centurion stood in front of the Redeemer. Recognizing that he was dead, he shoved his spear into the chest cavity (in fulfillment of prophecy, Psalms 22:16), then withdrew it. The gospel of John records that water and blood came forth from the wound (John 19:34). Elder James E. Talmage and others indicate that the watery serum separated from the blood because the Savior died of a ruptured cardiac, or in more common terms, a broken heart. His great heart literally burst as he offered himself, fully, a sacrifice for fallen man.

Having already felt such a deep sorrow for what happened to the Savior in Gethsemane and as he was scourged, the additional feelings that came as I pondered the crucifixion were almost more than I could bear. I thought, and again, this seems to be the key to an understanding of the atonement, that my own heart would break because of the sorrow I felt.

Because of the intensity of my feelings that night, especially because of what happened in the Garden of Gethsemane, there came into my mind an analogy. Bear in mind that this is only an analogy; yet perhaps it will help in sensing the reality and significance of what the Savior went through. Before commencing, let me add that one doesn't necessarily need to see the Lord or hear his voice to receive a remission of sins; however, obviously, that too could and does happen. In the analogy that follows, the idea of seeing and conversing with the Lord is used simply to emphasize the fact that as we become clean through his blood, we become overwhelmed by the realization that the Savior did suffer individually and personally for each one of us, and that because of that awareness on our part, we can and will feel a powerful, one-to-one commitment to and relationship with him.

Assume that although you have been a member of the Church and very active for a number of years, something has happened that causes you to take a fresh look at where you are in your relationship with the Savior and his gospel. You find yourself acquiring a much deeper hunger and thirst for the things of the Spirit which results in searching the scriptures a great deal, fasting like you have never fasted before, praying mightily many times a day, and increasing your fervor in your church callings.

Pursuing your quest, you become aware that there are innumerable promises in the scriptures that you can receive great power from the Lord, that marvelous knowledge and understanding can be yours, that revelation can be yours on a daily basis and that indeed the veil can become thin and even non-existent. But as you continue to seek with all the energy of your soul for the greater things of God, you find that the many promises of the Lord are not being realized in your life, and you wonder why. Again, the more you search the scriptures and fast and pray and give yourself in service, the greater is your desire to receive "all mysteries, yea all the hidden mysteries of my kingdom from days of old, and for ages to come." (D&C 76:7.)

Continuing to seek and desiring profoundly to know why you are not the recipient of greater heavenly power and blessings, all at once there comes into your mind the realization that you don't have the greater power because you are not totally clean—you have not been completely forgiven of your sins. The scriptures seem to make it abundantly clear that if you are free from sin, if you have genuinely been cleansed, your body will be a virtual temple of God, you will enjoy the Spirit on a daily basis, and you will grow in the spirit of revelation.

The realization comes with a suddenness and a clarity that, frankly, quite stuns you. Perhaps you have never sinned grossly (although that would not negate the possibility of complete forgiveness), and yet you are mindful that you have been very unkind on occasion, you have been jealous, short-tempered, not always honest, and not always filled with complete commitment. What stuns you further is that in all the years you have been a member of the Church you have never really, specifically and powerfully, pled for a complete remission of your sins. With all of the many steps of repentance, you have not sought for the mercy, merits, and grace of Christ to come upon you that you might be sanctified fully by his blood.

You determine, then, to seek with all of your heart for a remission of your sins. You realize that on top of keeping the commandments and carrying a heavy load of responsibility in church work, the *key* to receiving a remission of your sins will indeed be "mighty prayer." (D&C 29:1; Enos.)

As you persist in your quest, your hunger and thirst for righteousness become even more intense. You begin to feel you want a remission of your sins more than anything else in life. Because of your increased desire and persistence, your prayers become more effective. You look forward to lifting up your voice in prayer every chance you get.

Late one evening, after several months of diligently carrying out your plan, you find yourself concluding the day by calling vocally upon your Heavenly Father, seeking specifically for a remission of your sins. After pouring out your heart for an extended period of time, you become suddenly aware of a bright light in front of you. You open your eyes and there stands the Lord! What a glorious experience it is just to see him! He speaks, and as he does, each word distills an intensity of pure love to every cell of your body. "I have come to give you a remission of your sins," he says.

Your initial reaction is one of complete surprise. You are, in fact, startled to learn that a remission of sins comes directly from the Lord. Even though Nephi, Enos, Alma the younger, and for that matter all of the prophets, have testified that this is what happens, you somehow had not made that connection between receiving a remission of sins and the fact that it is given you by the Lord himself.

He speaks again: "In order for you to receive a remission of your sins, it is necessary that you and I walk back through the corridors of your life that we may review your past sins."

You are shocked at his invitation. You do not want to go back over your life with him. You have already turned away from your sins and you do not want to review them—especially with the Lord. Just being in his presence has had a quickening effect on your conscience and has already caused you to wince in remembrance of your sins. Yet even though you are overwhelmed at the prospect of a vivid review of your transgressions, because you have sought so diligently over an extended period of time to receive a remission of your sins, you feel you must have the strength and courage to face what you know will be a profoundly embarrassing review. And the Lord's presence gives you courage. You reach out your hand, the Savior takes it, and together you start walking back through the corridors of your life.

You are quite mindful of the sins you will see and you don't relish seeing them while standing beside your Redeemer. Your fears are confirmed as you see yourself down the corridor, yet some distance away, in an act of transgression. You gently tug on the Savior's hand and suggest you are close enough—that you can see fine from where you are. The Lord, however, reminds you that you must walk all the way up and face squarely the sins you have committed. In fact, as the Savior reminds you of that necessity, the many declarations of the prophets, both ancient and modern, as to the necessity of total confession flood into your mind.

So there you are, a personal witness with the Lord of your transgressions. Seeing yourself in the act of sinning causes an intensified sorrow to come into your heart, and there wells up within you an earnest yearning for the blood of Christ to atone for your personal transgressions. As you feel this great desire, many scriptural promises come vividly into your mind—such promises as "there shall be no other name given . . . whereby salvation can come unto the children of men" (Mosiah 3:17), and "there is no other way nor means whereby man can be saved, only through the atoning blood of Christ" (Helaman 5:9). With these scriptures and others pounding through your mind, you feel a hope coming into your heart. With great faith and feeling, you pray in effect, "Heavenly Father, I sense deeply the seriousness of my sins. I'm sorry for all that I have done that was wrong. I know your son, even Jesus Christ, is the Savior and Redeemer of the world, and I pray that I might be forgiven of my sins and cleansed by his blood."

Because you have been so intently pleading for mercy, you haven't noticed the Savior for several minutes. You become aware that he is no longer holding on to your hand, and you turn to look at him. Whereas his countenance had been one of joy and peace, you notice that now his face is etched with pain and sorrow. As you watch, he begins to tremble and sweat profusely. Gradually the water color of his sweat changes to a reddish hue, and you become aware that the little capillaries in his flesh are bursting and he begins to sweat great drops of blood out of every pore. And then you realize what is happening. He is suffering *because of you*! His blood is being shed for your personal transgressions, and he has taken upon his shoulders the effects of your sins. As you become so deeply aware of his suffering for you, you feel that your heart will break. The reality of the Lord's personal testimony in the Doctrine and Covenants is overwhelming:

> For behold, I, God, have suffered these things for all, that they might not suffer if they would repent; but if they would not repent they must suffer even as I; which suffering caused myself, even God, the greatest of all, to tremble because of pain, and to bleed at every pore, and to suffer both body and spirit—and would that I might not drink the bitter cup, and shrink—nevertheless, glory be to the Father, and I partook and finished my preparations unto the children of men. (D&C 19:16-19.)

Suddenly you become aware that the sorrow and pain are being lifted out of you. As the effects of your sins are taken away, every cell of your body seems quickened with a new-found aliveness and your entire being tingles with a wonderful sense of innocence and cleanliness. Perhaps the best way to describe the joy, the peace, the aliveness, and especially the new-found love you are experiencing is to say simply, but with all the power of your soul, "Behold I am born of the Spirit." (Mosiah 27:24.) In addition, as you become so deeply aware of what it has taken for you to be forgiven of your sins and of the love both the Father and the Son have for you in being willing to have Christ suffer so deeply for you, there comes to you an overpowering awareness of your self-worth—a kind of celestial self-esteem.

The experience is now over. You return to the regular activities of life. But now you are constantly aware of the significance of the Savior's atonement; it has become the greatest reality of your life, as well as the central theme of all you say and do. You find great motivation and ability to keep the commandments because you have been endowed with such a marvelous increase of his love. You treat everyone in a Christlike way. You have a passion to do all in your power to bring others to the Father through Christ. You want to do all in your power to build the kingdom of God. And again, the central theme of your life is the graciousness of a loving God named Jehovah who loved you so much that he was willing to pay the terrible price that you might be free from sin.

I believe that herein lies the great message of the gospel as taught in the restored Church—in arriving at a point where we feel deeply the personal implications of the Savior's sorrow, suffering, and death. We grasp the message as we recognize the seriousness of the fallen condition we are in, the unbending demands of justice, and yet the fact that we can partake of the mercy and love of a divine Redeemer who is our advocate with the Father.

How vital it is to seek with all of our hearts for a revealed understanding of the atonement. As we search the scriptures, fast and pray, and give ourselves in untiring service in the building of the kingdom of God, we must be ever mindful that our lives and the lives of others will be blessed and endowed with mighty power only as we and they come to a heart-felt, revealed understanding of the atonement of Christ.

The following experience of President Joseph Fielding Smith sums up most effectively what I'm trying to say about the personal feelings that come as we learn by revelation of the importance of the Savior's sorrow and suffering:

> As children, so frequently we would hear him say, 'If only the people in the world would understand the trials, the tribulations, the sins our Lord took upon himself for our benefit.' Whenever he would refer to this, tears would come into his eyes.
>
> A few years ago, as I sat alone with my father in his study, I observed that he had been in deep meditation. I hesitated to break the silence, but finally he spoke. 'Oh my son, I wish you could have been with me last Thursday as I met with my Brethren in the temple. Oh, if you could have heard them testify of their love for their Lord and Savior, Jesus Christ!' And then he lowered his head and tears streamed from his face and dropped to his shirt. Then, after many seconds, without as much as

raising his head, but moving his head back and forth, he said, 'Oh how I love my Lord and Savior Jesus Christ!' (*New Era*, January 1972.) Joseph Fielding Smith as quoted by his son in the article "President Joseph Fielding Smith: Student of the Gospel," pp. 61-65. Quote p. 63.

Chapter 5

To Know The Lord Is To Know That Through The Second Birth We Can Become Like Him

Having discussed the atonement in the last chapter, concluding that the source of the Savior's redemptive power is his atoning sacrifice, let's now concentrate on the idea that the full enjoyment of the power of the atonement can be made available in our lives only if we are born again or baptized of the fire and the Holy Ghost. Receiving a testimony of the restored gospel and being willing to go into the waters of baptism in order to receive the gift of the Holy Ghost are marvelous things in the lives of all of us; but the greater, more challenging experience is to seek for and obtain the baptism of the Spirit. We need to know clearly that the second birth will not occur unless we as members of the Church "continue to humble ourselves before God, hungering and thirsting after righteousness, and living by every word that proceeds from the mouth of God." (DHC 3:380.) If we do that, we will grow in the

101

intensity of the Holy Ghost, we will be totally immersed in the heavenly element of the Spirit, and because of the baptism of the fire, we will overcome the evils of this life and lose every desire for sin. Achieving and maintaining the second birth is one of the greatest experiences of mortality and requires greater effort and determination than most of us realize; in addition, while it is true one can be baptized of the Spirit at the time the gift of the Holy Ghost is given, with most of us the second birth probably follows an extended period of time, depending on the effort of the individual candidate.

It is therefore my personal conviction that the greatest need we have as members of the Church is to be born again, to be sure that we have partaken so totally of the divine nature of Christ (2nd Peter 1:20)—that is, we have received the Savior's kindness, patience, sensitivity, and love through the endowments of the Holy Ghost—that it can be said of us that we are the sons and daughters of Christ. We need to recognize that the first fruit of true repentance is water baptism, and that if we will then fulfill the commandments, we will enjoy a total and complete remission of sins (Moroni 8:25).

Terms that Define Being Born Again

There are a number of terms the Lord and the prophets use to describe the experience of being born again. Each term is uniquely descriptive and adds to our understanding of that most important event. As a partial example: To be born again is referred to as becoming sanctified by the blood of Christ (Moses 6:60), or being made pure and spotless (Alma 13:12). It is referred to as being quickened in the inner man (Moses 6:65), and as baptism of the fire and the Holy Ghost (2 Nephi 31:13). Individuals who have been born again are said to have been spiritually begotten of Christ and are called his sons and daughters (Mosiah 5:7). Perhaps one of the most common terms to describe the experience of being born again is the term "converted" (4 Nephi 2). Being born again is also synonomous with a remission of sins (Alma 38:8).

Let me make an observation about the term "baptism of the fire." When we sin, our bodies and our spirits become contaminated, impure, and unholy. When we receive the baptism of the fire, the cleansing influence of the Spirit comes upon us with such intensity that the impurities are literally burned out of our bodies and we become sanctified and made clean. As the Savior indicated, we are healed and made whole (2 Nephi 16:10), thus preparing our bodies for the regular daily companionship of the Holy Ghost.

Responding to the Savior's Call

In October Conference of 1961, much attention had been given to correlating all of the studies and activities of the Priesthood with the auxiliaries of the Church. In the priesthood session, President David O. McKay, in an effort to give proper focus to the correlation efforts of the Church, asked an important question: "What is the end and purpose of all this?" Answering his own question, he said that there was but "one great purpose in mind, and that is to fulfill or respond to that call that Jesus gave to Nicodemus: '... Except a man be born of the water and the spirit, he cannot enter into the Kingdom of God.' (John 3:5.)" (David O. McKay, CR October1961, p. 89.)

What an awesome challenge the Lord has given the Church—to make sure that the Priesthood and all of its programs, the Relief Society organization, Sunday School, and all other meetings and programs are organized and directed in such a way that the membership of the Church achieve the great goal of having their lives transformed through the experience of the second birth.

It's exciting to see how Alma set about to assist the saints in his day. When he became aware that many were slipping into inactivity and even apostasy, he saw clearly that there was "no way he might reclaim them save it be in bearing down in pure testimony against them" (Alma 4:19), and the program he launched and the testimony he bore was in the query, "Have ye spiritually been born of God?" (Alma 5:14.)

Peter the apostle had an interesting problem that is not uncommon to most of us. He knew Jesus was the Christ, but he did not have the power to honor that testimony fully. At Caesarea Phillipi Peter responded to the Savior's inquiring as to who he, Christ, was by declaring, "Thou art the Christ, the son of the living God." (Matthew 16:16.) Almost three years later he boldly said he would be willing to go with Christ to prison and even to death (Luke 22:33), and yet within hours after that last promise, he denied his beloved Savior three times. Peter's ability to serve the Lord in power and integrity came on the day of Pentecost, when in fulfillment of a promise of the Savior that he would be converted or born again (Luke 22:32), the blessed event occurred and what power he then possessed!

Even the original twelve apostles of our dispensation, after serving in that holy calling for three years, were promised that "if they harden not their hearts, and stiffen not their necks against me, they shall be converted, and I will heal them." (D&C 112:13.) If such was the case with Peter and some of the original Twelve, oh how anxious we should be to make sure the baptism of the fire and Holy Ghost occurs in our lives!

The Conception and the Birth

As indicated earlier, generally the baptism of the Spirit does not occur immediately with the baptism of the water; usually it takes some time to search the scriptures adequately, to develop the ability to live by the Spirit sufficiently, to render the needed service to our fellowmen. The gradual preparation for the second birth is likened to the process of mortal birth. In mortal birth, there is the conception, the gestation period, and then the birth. Perhaps we could see baptism of the water as the conception of the new son or daughter of Christ, the period of growth in faith and service as the gestation period, and then when we are immersed fully in the power of the Holy Ghost, we issue forth a son or daughter of Christ.

I know in my own life that at eight when I was baptized, the main thing that occurred was my becoming a member of the Church and receiving the right to the Spirit and power of the Holy Ghost. I didn't seek diligently for the Spirit until I was 19, and then the spiritual process began to occur. Some time after that, greater spiritual changes occurred and the more complete assurance was mine that the Lord had truly changed my life.

The Mighty Change

In the scriptures we find many beautiful examples of the second birth: Paul, Alma the younger, the 300 Lamanites, Lamoni and his wife and many others. However, most of these examples seem unusually dramatic and some wonder if it is really fair to use them to show how people are born again. It is indeed a disservice to insist that one must have a dramatic experience (angels appearing, voices heard, etc.) in order to be born again—such is not the case. Yet, I think it's important to realize that one can have a marvelous veil-thinning experience in knowing one is forgiven of their sins. To reject that possibility is to take away from the credibility of the scriptures and many beautiful experiences the saints have had in our dispensation. But whether our greater conversion occurs dramatically or as "the wind bloweth" and we do not know from whence it comes (John 3:8), the results are the same—we have experienced a mighty change of heart.

Joseph F. Smith told of the quiet but powerful experience he had after his baptism:

The feeling that came upon me was that of pure peace, of love and of light. I felt in my soul that if I had sinned—and surely I was not without sin—that it had been forgiven me; that I was indeed cleansed from sin; my heart was touched and I felt that I would not injure the smallest insect beneath my feet. I felt as though I wanted to do good everywhere to everybody and to everything. I felt a newness of life, a newness of desire to do that which was right. (Joseph F. Smith, *CR* April 1898, p. 66.)

Heber C. Kimball recorded that after he came up out of the water and was confirmed, he "received the Holy Ghost, as the disciples did in ancient days, which was like a consuming fire. I felt as though I sat at the feet of Jesus." (Orson F. Whitney, *Life of Heber C. Kimball*, Salt Lake City, Kimball Family, 1888, p. 39.)

President Lorenzo Snow relates a beautiful experience somewhat more dramatic in nature:

Some two or three weeks after I was baptized, one day while engaged in my studies, I began to reflect upon the fact that I had not obtained a knowledge of the truth of the work . . . and I began to feel very uneasy. I laid aside my books, left the house, and wandered around through the fields under the oppressive influence of a gloomy, disconsolate spirit, while an indescribable cloud of darkness seemed to envelop me. I had been accustomed at the close of the day to retire for secret prayer . . . but at this time I felt no inclination to do so. . . . At length, realizing that the usual time had come for secret prayer, I concluded I would not forego my evening service, and, as a matter of formality, knelt as I was in the habit of doing, and in my accustomed retired place, but not feeling as I was wont to feel.

I had no sooner opened my lips in an effort to pray than I heard a sound, just above my head, like the rustling of silken robes, and immediately the Spirit of God descended upon me, completely enveloping my whole person, filling me, from the crown of my head to the soles of my feet, and O, the joy and happiness I felt! No language can describe the almost instantaneous transition from a dense cloud of mental and spiritual darkness into a refulgence of light and knowledge, as it was at that time imparted to my understanding. I then received a perfect knowledge that God lives, that Jesus Christ is the Son of God, and of the restoration. . . . It was a complete baptism—a tangible immersion in the heavenly principle or element, the Holy Ghost; and even more real and physical in its effects upon every part of my system than the immersion by water; dispelling forever, so long as reason and memory last, all possibility of doubt. . . .

I cannot tell how long I remained in the full flow of the blissful enjoyment and divine enlightenment, but it was several minutes before the celestial element which filled and surrounded me began gradually to withdraw. On arising from my kneeling posture, . . . I knew that He had conferred on me what only an omnipotent being can confer—that which is of greater value than all the wealth and honors worlds can bestow. That night, as I retired to rest, the same wonderful manifestations were repeated, and continued to be for several successive nights. The sweet remembrance of those glorious experiences . . . impart[s] an inspiring influence to me . . . and I trust will be the close of my earthly existence. (*Biography and Family Record of Lorenzo Snow*, comp. Eliza R. Snow, Salt Lake City: Deseret Book Co., 1884, pp. 7-9.)

An experience out of the Book of Mormon showing a marvelous outpouring of the spirit following an extended preparation, is the experience King Benjamin had with his subjects. The saints had gathered together to hear their prophet-king Benjamin. The saints who gathered on that occasion appear in many ways similar to the good, active members of the Church today. They had achieved, through the gospel, freedom from dissension and war, they kept the commandments, they prospered economically, and how they loved, respected, and adored their prophet!

These Nephites lived in a general condition of "goodness." However, as King Benjamin began to speak to them, one of the first things he emphasized was that he wanted to call them together "that I might be found blameless, and that your blood should not come upon me, when I shall stand to be judged of God of the things whereof he hath commanded me concerning you." (Mosiah 2:28.) He also indicated that he wanted to give them a new name (Mosiah 1:11.)

King Benjamin, by the power of the spoken word, went on to lead his people to new heights in achieving Christlike character. He opened a whole new world to a precious group of people who were already remarkably good in their obedience to God. How did he do it? How was he able to get the people to realize there was so much more to their membership in the Church than that which they were enjoying?

First, he stressed the tremendous importance of service: "When ye are in the service of your fellow beings ye are only in the service of your God." (Mosiah 2:17.) Second, he acknowledged in such a kind, positive way his appreciation for the reverence and love his subjects manifested so visibly for him. However, at the same time he cautioned them in their adoration of him and lifted their sights measureably by teaching them that if he as their earthly king merited any thanks, "O how you ought to thank your heavenly King!" (Mosiah 2:19.)

Third, and he did this so delicately and yet powerfully, King Benjamin set about to bring his people to a deep sense of humility that they might be in a position to be lifted to much greater heights. He did this by stressing the idea that they, for all their goodness, for all their diligence in keeping the commandments, for all their determination to be of service to one another, were simply unprofitable servants; so unprofitable, in fact, that they were less than the dust of the earth! (Mosiah 2:25.)

Fourthly, King Benjamin was apparently given a marvelous ability to help his subjects understand the majesty of the atonement of Christ. Somehow, even though the people were very active in the gospel and were performing many "good works," they hadn't yet comprehended that it would take the power of God to "put off the natural man." (Mosiah 3:19.) The Savior as their Redeemer hadn't yet become the very center of their lives, his power hadn't yet transformed their fallen nature. Consequently, speaking words given him by an angel the night before, the prophet king delivered a remarkably powerful sermon which centered in the necessity of the atonement of Christ.

How well prepared were the hearts of the people for the delicious words of eternal life! In fact, as their prophet testified of the mighty works Christ would perform, of the terrible temptations, pain, hunger, thirst, fatigue he would endure, and of his great anguish which would cause blood to come from every pore, the people of King Benjamin fell to the earth; for they:

> viewed themselves in their own carnal state, even less than the dust of the earth. And they all cried aloud with one voice, saying: O have mercy, and apply the atoning blood of Christ that we may receive forgiveness of our sins, and our hearts may be purified; for we believe in Jesus Christ, the Son of God, who created heaven and earth, and all things; who shall come down among the children of men. (Mosiah 4:2.)

After the people of King Benjamin cried out for mercy, "the Spirit of the Lord came upon them and they were filled with joy, having received a remission of their sins, and having peace of conscience, because of the exceeding faith which they had in Jesus Christ who should come, according to the words which King Benjamin had spoken unto them (Mosiah 4:3).

In addition, they all possessed an abhorrence for sin and wanted to do good continually (5:2), and they possessed a desire to share their worldly goods. They also learned that now they were truly born again, if they desired to maintain that great condition, they could do so if they "must retain in remembrance the greatness of God, and your own nothingness, and his goodness and long-suffering towards you, unworthy creatures, and humble yourselves even in the depths of humility, calling on the name of the Lord daily, and standing steadfastly in the faith of that which is to come (Mosiah 4:11).

I love the experience of King Benjamin—here we have a whole group of people who came to a marvelous personal knowledge of the atonement of the Savior, and in so doing obtained sufficient faith to become spiritually begotten of Christ. They, having received so totally of the divine nature of Christ, became his sons and his daughters and now enjoyed, not just theoretically, but in a marvelous, real way, the sacred name of their Redeemer, even Jesus Christ (5:7).

One of the greatest sermons on the second birth is Nephi's discourse in chapters 31 and 32 of 2 Nephi. In fact, it is my personal opinion that these two chapters shed more light on what it means to enjoy the second birth than any other single sermon in all of Holy Writ. I would recommend strongly that you study carefully and prayerfully these two very illuminating chapters.

Getting Through the Gate and on the Path

When I was baptized at eight and confirmed a member of the Church, I assumed I had "entered the gate and obtained the path." Nephi would disagree. He indicates we haven't gone through the gate and obtained the path until we are baptized of the fire and the Holy Ghost (31:17). In fact, Nephi testifies that the baptism of the fire and the Holy Ghost is so marvelous that if after receiving it we should deny Christ, it would have been better had we never known him (31:14). Such warning is usually reserved for those who could be candidates for becoming sons of perdition (Matthew 26:24).

Nephi makes some important observations about "following the example of Christ." First of all, he explains that we must follow him into the waters of baptism and, like him, be baptized of the fire and the Holy Ghost. Secondly, we must endure to the end in following Christ's example (2 Nephi 31:16). In other words, it is one thing to get on the straight and narrow path and another thing to live out our lives in following Christ's example. This latter requirement is achieved through "feasting on the words of Christ," which we will discuss later.

The efficacy of baptism, like that of all ordinances of the gospel, depends upon our attitude, preparation, and faith in Christ. *If*, Nephi says, there is no hypocrisy, no deception, real repentance, and one is truly willing to take upon themselves the name of Christ (31:13), then and only then will the baptism of fire and the Holy Ghost occur. We should all understand that if, when we were baptized, we did not meet all the above qualifications, as soon as we do, our baptism will become valid and effective.

"By Their Fruits Ye Shall Know Them"

I think the Lord is anxious for us to know exactly where we stand in terms of fulfilling our covenants and commitments to him. He doesn't want us to wonder from day to day if we are acceptable to him. This is particularly true of the covenant of baptism. He has told us exactly what he expects of us and that if we will take upon ourselves his name, keep all of his commandments, always remember him, bear one another's burdens and stand as a witness of him at all times (Mosiah 18:9), then we can expect without qualification to be forgiven of our sins, receive the gift and daily guidance of the Holy Ghost and obtain while yet in the flesh the promise of eternal life if we continue faithful.

The Savior, so many times, indicated that "by their fruits ye shall know them" (Matthew 7:16), and we can know if we are truly born again by our fruits. What are the hallmarks of one who is spiritually begotten by Christ? Nephi discusses five important characteristics we will enjoy if we are really on the straight and narrow path.

Speaking With the Tongues of Angels

The first thing Nephi said would happen to us if we are baptized of the fire and the Holy Ghost is that we would "speak with the tongues of angels" (31:13). He then tells us that to do so is to speak under the influence and power of the Holy Ghost (32:2-3). It seems so natural, so logical that one who has tasted fully of the transforming power of God would enjoy the privilege of speaking by the power of the Holy Ghost. You and I have acquired our faith in Christ primarily because we have heard the testimonies of others who spoke words charged with the heavenly element of the Holy Ghost. The Lord is anxious that we, like them, be instruments in testifying to others of the marvelous truths we have learned. To speak with the tongues of angels is continually to speak words of comfort, encouragement, and love. It is to teach by the Spirit and to reflect in all we say the inspiration and power of the Lord.

I'm sure all of us from time to time have felt the indescribable thrill of saying things that we knew at the time came directly from the Lord—we know the power such words can carry in everything we say.

One example of enjoying the ability to speak with the power of the Spirit was a special teaching moment I had with three daughters ages 3, 4, and 5. At the time this experience occurred I was babysitting. The children seemed to be in an unusually receptive spirit, so I decided to tell them the story of the brother of Jared. We got the eight barges built, solved the air problem, and then I indicated that the brother of Jared went up on the mountain with sixteen transparent stones that the Lord might touch them and provide light for the voyage.

I told them how fervently the brother of Jared prayed, and that he saw the finger of the Lord. Speaking in a quiet, subdued manner I said simply, "And then, children, because of the faith of the brother of Jared, the Savior appeared to him and talked with him. At that moment I glanced down and noticed our five-year-old looking up at me with tears just streaming down her face and she said, "Oh Daddy, that's just beautiful, that's just beautiful!" And then with continued great feeling she said, "Daddy, some day I've just got to see Jesus, I've just got to see him!" Oh, how that touched my heart. There was no question my precious daughter knew through the Spirit that the story I was telling her was true. At least in part, perhaps that is what speaking with the tongues of angels is all about.

Shouting Praises to the Holy One of Israel

Another characteristic we enjoy through the second birth is wanting to "shout praises to the Holy One of Israel" (31:13). Although Nephi does not elaborate on this characteristic, I think it is obvious what he is having reference to. I would like to believe that one of the great common denominators among all saints who have tasted of the goodness of Christ, who have felt "to sing the song of redeeming love" (Alma 5:26), would be to stand unashamedly as a witness of Christ at all times, and in all things, and in all places (Mosiah 18:9); not as a casual witness, or one who merely spoke frequently the Master's name, but rather one who would "shout" by his life, his words, and his deeds, that the Savior is his Redeemer and that through him life has incredible meaning.

We are commanded to hold up the Savior as our light. How natural it is to spontaneously hold him up when indeed he is our light. A city that is set on a hill cannot be hid (Matthew 5:14);

neither is it possible for a Latter-day Saint filled with the light and power of the Savior to move among the children of men without their knowing that Christ is the source of his light.

To shout praises to the Holy One of Israel is portrayed powerfully in what the Lord says about what the faithful will do when he comes in his glory; for the faithful will continually "mention the loving kindness of their Lord, and all that he has bestowed upon them according to his goodness and according to his loving kindness forever and ever." (D&C 133:52.)

To "shout praises to the Holy One of Israel" is a great hallmark of true conversion. The ability to so shout is a gift which comes through the ordinances as a result of mighty faith in Christ, and in that shout, the central object is Christ and the central message is that he is our personal Redeemer.

Possessing a Perfect Hope

Nephi indicates that being on the straight and narrow, we must press forward with a steadfastness in Christ, having a perfect brightness of hope (31:20). I think having a perfect brightness of hope is to enjoy the consistent assurance from the Savior through the Spirit that we will inherit everlasting life. To possess a perfect hope is more than simply to have a lively desire, for hope arises from a righteous heart and again it is a confidence, born of the Spirit, that one will inherit exaltation. The prophet Mormon said of hope, "And what is it that ye shall hope for? Behold I say unto you that ye shall have hope through the atonement of Christ and the power of his resurrection, to be raised unto life eternal." (Moroni 8:41.) With all due respect to the joy of earth life and its eternal significance, I think it is most natural to "hope" someday to be carried beyond this vale of sorrow into a far better land of promise (Alma 37:45). Moroni said it so well when he said, "Wherefore whoso believeth in God might with surety hope for a better world, yea, even a place at the right hand of God, which hope cometh of faith, maketh an anchor to the souls of men, which would make them sure and steadfast, always abounding in good works, being led to glorify God." (Ether 12:4.)

To Love God and All Men

To have been baptized of the fire and the Holy Ghost is to be an heir or possessor of charity, the pure love of Christ. All the examples of men and women who are truly born again reflect without exception that marvelous quality. Now, Nephi declares that having obtained the path and being steadfast in Christ, we will have "a love of God and of all men" (2 Nephi 31:20).

As the Spirit works with us we are quite amazed, ofttimes, at how strongly we feel about others, how strongly we love them, not because we should love them but simply because we do. I know I have been caught off guard, so to speak, with the feelings of love for others that have come on different occasions and I know it is because of him and not simply my own doing.

One such occasion occurred while driving from Los Angeles to Ridgecrest, California, for a lecture. It was a beautiful spring day and as I drove across the desert, I noticed up ahead on my right a dirt hill about five-hundred feet high. There were a half dozen or so "souped-up" cars maneuvering all over the hill. I decided to stop and watch their antics. As I got out of my car to get a better view and also to enjoy the California sun, I noticed there was a car parked about forty feet behind me, and standing in front of the car were a fellow and a girl. They looked like they were in their late teens and judging by the way they were dressed and just their overall appearance, I concluded they were way off the path—in fact, I decided they probably didn't even know there was a path!

After watching the cars for a few minutes, I glanced at my watch and knew I must be hurrying on. As I turned to get in the car, I glanced back and noticed the fellow was still standing there watching, but the girl had gotten in the car. Right at that moment I felt strongly impressed to walk back and chat with the young man.

I quickly introduced myself and asked him a couple of questions that I hoped would cause him to ask who I was, which they did. I told him who I was and that I taught in the Religion Department at Brigham Young University. He got a little bit of a funny look in his eyes and responded with, "Oh, you must be a Mormon." I said, "Yes, I am." He paused for a moment and then a little apologetically said, "Well, I am too." Then I knew why I had been so impressed to introduce myself to him. Immediately I felt such a strong love for that fellow. I reached up, put my hand on the back of his neck, pulled him closer to me, rested my forearm on his chest and quickly told him my feelings about the Lord, how grateful I was for the Church and how completely my life had been changed because of my relationship with the Savior. The words came so easily! I wasn't preachy, but I came on strong and he was so receptive. His eyes glistened with excitement and gratitude as he told me how much he appreciated what I was saying. Again, looking at my watch, I knew I had to hurry, so I pulled my hand and arm away, but he caught hold of my hand and just kept saying, "Thanks, thanks so much." How I wanted to put him in the car and take him home and get him back on the path! Anyway, it was a beautiful experience and I couldn't help but acknowledge that the feeling of love came from above.

Feasting on the Words of Christ

The final characteristic Nephi speaks about is that of "feasting on the words of Christ," which really teaches us powerfully why being baptized of the fire and the Holy Ghost is such a marvelous, experience and it has to do again with following the example of Christ.

Nephi, perhaps because he speaks so plainly, almost sounds both blunt and casual as he explains what it means to "feast upon the words of Christ." He says simply, "the words of Christ will tell you *all* things what ye should do." (2 Nephi 32:3.) He recognizes that we probably didn't understand what he meant because we hadn't knocked or asked (32:4), so he says it again! "I say unto you that if you will enter in by the way, and receive the Holy Ghost, it will show unto you *all* things what ye should do." (32:5.)

I wish I had the power to express what a tremendous impact Nephi's teachings on living by the Spirit has had on my life. I know that the same doctrine of living under the constant companionship of the Spirit is spelled out beautifully in the sacrament prayer—that is, if we remember the Lord, his Spirit will be with us always. I know that if the Savior is the examplar for all of us to follow and he took his directions or cues from the Father constantly, that we, in following his example, will try to take our directions or cues from the Savior constantly. Yet somehow I grew up in the Church not really believing that I have the obligation and responsibility to so live my life that Jesus Christ will, through the Spirit, be my constant companion, that in that relationship he, through the Spirit, will show me all the things that I should do!

In fact, for some strange reason, I picked up the idea that when the Lord said, "Behold it is not meet that I should command in all things" (D&C 58:26), that what he meant was that I was not to expect the constant companionship of the Holy Ghost, that I was not to expect the Lord's help in all my decisions, that I was not to look to Christ in every thought (D&C 6:36)—I didn't know that when he said " . . .men should be anxiously engaged in a good cause, and do many things of their own free will, and bring to pass much righteousness; for the power is in them" (D&C 58:27-28), that the power is the power of the Holy Ghost! Oh, how I missed the point, and, oh, how many blessings I missed because of that misunderstanding. To know that we are commanded to so live that the Holy Ghost can tell us all things that we should do, is the very key to moving along the straight and narrow path to ultimate perfection. In fact, it is the only way we can be saved.

Certainly, it's hard to live by the Spirit on a regular basis; certainly it's hard to wrestle and struggle with the decisions we make hoping to get the necessary confirmation that the decisions we make are correct. It may seem hard to believe that we can arrive at a point where all the decisions we make are correct, but, I believe, to truly follow the example of Christ and to feast upon the words of Christ means we ultimately can arrive at a point where we need not make mistakes!

Throughout the scriptures, we find a number of other indicators which help us know if we are born of the Spirit. Including the five Nephi gives us, let's summarize the major ones:

(1) We will have experienced a broken heart and contrite spirit (D&C 20:37). One can't come to a revealed understanding of the atonement without sensing profoundly his inadequacies and sins, without sensing deeply his total dependency on the Lord to the point that his heart is broken and his spirit is contrite. We will remember the "greatness of God, and [our] own nothingness, and his goodness and longsuffering towards [us], unworthy creatures, and humble [ourselves] even in the depths of humility." (Mosiah 4:11.)

(2) We will have an overwhelming daily awareness of Christ and his marvelous atonement. We will "root" what we say and teach, as well as our labors in the kingdom in the central reality of Christ's atoning sacrifice. We will "shout praises to the Holy One of Israel" (2 Nephi 31:13) and will "stand as a witness of God [Christ] at all times and in all things, and in all places." (Mosiah 18:9.)

(3) We will look upon sin with abhorrence (Alma 13:12) and have no disposition to do evil (Mosiah 5:2; 2 Nephi 9:49). Movies (R and X rated, and many rated PG!), literature, and TV, (regardless of how artistically they are done!) and all things that partake of

the grossness and sensuality of the world will clearly be repugnant to us.

(4) We will have a profound love of God and all men. We will sense the infinite worth of all of our Heavenly Father's children and do all in our power to treat everyone with whom we come in contact in a Christlike way.

(5) Our very nature will be changed. As President McKay put it, "Human nature must be changed on an enormous scale in the future unless the world is to be drowned in its own blood, and only Christ can change it." (David O. McKay, *CR* October 1953, p. 11.) With our nature changed, our very personality will become more like the Savior's. "Those who have got the forgiveness of their sins have the countenances that look bright, and they shine with the intelligence of heaven." (Brigham Young, *Times and Seasons*, 6:956.) "When the will, passions, and feelings of a person are perfectly submissive to God and his requirements, that person is sanctified." (Brigham Young, *JD* 2:123.)

(6) Our great drive in life will be to do all in our power to bring individuals to the Father through Christ. We will be willing to make whatever effort and sacrifice is necessary to possess the power to encourage people to repent and live the gospel.

(7) We will be free with our temporal goods (Mosiah 4:16). We will pay our tithes, be generous in our fast offerings and live the spirit of the law of consecration (4 Nephi 3).

(8) We will have prophetic views of that which is to come (Mosiah 4:41). We will look forward to the second coming (D&C 45:39).

(9) We will desire with all of our hearts to live by the Spirit: "For as many as are led by the Spirit of God, they are the sons of God." (Romans 8:14.)

(10) We will speak with the tongues of angels (2 Nephi 32:2).

(11) We won't allow our children to quarrel (Mosiah 4:14).

(12) We will see in a mighty way the mantle of divine authority resting on the Lord's anointed and we will be willing to receive

their words as if from the mouth of the Lord (D&C 21:5).

(13) We will remember the sins we have committed but there will be no pain associated with that memory (Alma 36:19).

(14) We will be filled with peace and have a perfect hope (2 Nephi 31:20). We will know our hearts are right and that we desire righteousness and are acceptable to the Lord. President Lee shared the following experience about knowing when one is born again and the attendant peace that follows:

> Brother Romney and I were sitting in the office one day and a young missionary came in. He was getting ready to go on a mission, and he had been interviewed in the usual way and had made confessions of certain transgressions of his youth, but he said to us, "I'm not satisfied by just having confessed. How can I know that I have been forgiven?" In other words, "How do I know that I am born again?"
>
> Brother Romney said to him again, "My son, you wait and pray until you have the peace of conscience."

(15) We will see ourselves as a "babe in Christ"; that is, we will realize that having been "quickened in the inner man" (Moses 6:65), we are on the threshold of great spiritual growth and development; but we will be aware that there is much to learn, much yet to do and become before we can put on the full stature of Christ. We will also realize that once we are born again, we may yet fall from the grace of God and lose our standing with him (D&C 20:30-31).

Those Who Are Truly Born Again

President McKay, as a young man, was sailing to the Samoan Islands on a Church assignment. A particularly beautiful sunset and a series of ideas and reflections seemed to prepare him for a remarkable experience that taught him ever so powerfully of the importance of being born again. He records:

> Toward evening, the reflection of the afterglow of a
> beautiful sunset was most splendid! The sky was tinged
> with pink, and the clouds lingering around the horizon
> were fringed with various hues of crimson and orange,
> while the heavy cloud farther to the west was somber
> purple and black. These colors cast varying shadows on
> the peaceful surface of the water. Those from the cloud
> were long and dark, those from the crimson-tinged sky,
> clear but rose tinted and fading into a beautiful calm
> twilight that made the sea look like a great mirror upon
> which fell the faint light of the crescent moon.
>
> Pondering still upon this beautiful scene, I lay in berth
> at ten o'clock that night and thought to myself: Charming
> as it is, it doesn't stir my soul with emotion as do the
> innocent lives of children, and the sublime characters of
> loved ones and friends. Their beauty, unselfishness, and
> heroism are, after all, the most glorious!
>
> I then fell asleep, and beheld in vision something
> infinitely sublime. In the distance I beheld a beautiful
> white city. Though it was far away, yet I seemed to
> realize the trees with luscious fruit, shrubbery with
> gorgeously tinted leaves, and flowers in perfect bloom
> abounded everywhere. The clear sky above seemed to
> reflect these beautiful shades of color. I then saw a great
> concourse of people approaching the city. Each one wore
> a white flowing robe and white headdress. Instantly my
> attention seemed centered upon their leader, and
> though I could see only the profile of his features and his
> body, I recognized him at once as my Savior! The tint
> and radiance of his countenance were glorious to
> behold. There was a peace about him which seemed
> sublime—it was divine!
>
> The city, I understood, was his. It was the City Eternal;
> and the people following him were to abide there in

peace and eternal happiness.

But who were they?

As if the Savior read my thoughts, he answered by pointing to a semicircle that then appeared above them, and on which were written in gold the words:

These Are They Who Have Overcome the World—
Who Have Truly Been Born Again!

When I awoke, it was breaking day over Apia harbor. (Claire Middlemiss, comp., *Cherished Experiences*, Salt Lake City: Deseret Book, 1976, pp. 59-60.)

Thirty-nine years later, President McKay pled with the members of the Church,

May God grant that members of the Church everywhere resist temptations that weaken the body, that destroy the soul, that we may be born again; that our souls might bask in the light of the Holy Spirit, and go on as true members of the Church of Jesus Christ until our mission on earth is completed (David O. McKay, *CR* April 1960, p. 29.)

The experience the Lord has ordained to change our lives and prepare us for entrance into the celestial kingdom is the second birth. If that experience occurs, we will be forgiven of our sins, our nature will be changed, and we will enjoy the daily companionship of the Holy Ghost. Because of the companionship of the Spirit, our love for everyone will be godly, and we will come to know the Lord and Savior Jesus Christ in a marvelous way and be pleased to dedicate our lives to the building of the kingdom of God.

Chapter 6

To Know The Lord Is To Know We Can Live Under His Daily Influence By And Through The Holy Ghost

We should all seek to be spiritually born of God that in becoming free from sin and having our nature changed, we might enjoy the marvelous companionship of the Holy Ghost, grow in the knowledge and stature of Christ, and receive the Savior's guidance in our daily lives. When we are born again we are babes in Christ, standing as it were at the threshold of unlimited knowledge, capable of becoming in time a man or woman of Christ in the fullest sense of the word. The primary element in our growth toward perfection is the Spirit, and our primary goal should be to live daily under the influence and power of the Holy Ghost.

A number of years ago a prominent singer/entertainer, one who was heavily involved in a protestant movement, came to BYU to speak at a devotional assembly in the old Smith Fieldhouse. A tremendous personality, the guest speaker began his address by saying, in effect, "I can't see that you Mormons believe a lot differently than I do except you keep talking about the Holy Ghost!" I was high in the upper levels of the Fieldhouse and it was all I could do to restrain myself from jumping up and yelling, "Hey! That's the whole difference!"

While what I wanted to say was perhaps a bit oversimplified, it really does sum up quite well the main difference between the restored Church and all other churches on earth. The fact that we actually possess the gift and power of the Holy Ghost is what makes the restored Church distinctively divine. The Holy Ghost is what sets us apart. President Martin Van Buren once asked the Prophet Joseph wherein Mormonism was different than other religions of the day. Joseph wrote later that he had told President Van Buren that "we differed in mode of baptism, and the gift of the Holy Ghost by the laying on of hands. *We considered that all other considerations were contained in the gift of the Holy Ghost.*" (DHC 4:42; emphasis added.)

The Holy Ghost is the very connecting link between God and man enabling man to possess the very powers of heaven. Although we often speak of many different manifestations of the power of God such as the power of faith, the power of the priesthood and so forth, in a very real sense essentially all power manifested by God to man is by and through the Holy Ghost.

"The Holy Ghost takes of the Father, and of the Son, and shows it to the disciples. It shows them things past, present, and to come. It opens the vision of the mind, unlocks the treasures of wisdom, and they begin to understand the things of God; ... it leads them to drink at the fountain of eternal wisdom, justice, and truth; they grow in grace, and in the knowledge of the truth as it is in Jesus Christ, until they see as they are seen, and know as they are known. (JD Brigham Young 1:241.)

It is the Holy Ghost that enables us to be patient, longsuffering, gentle and meek (D&C 121:41-42). It is the Holy Ghost that enables us to be gently persuasive in a Christlike way. It is the Holy Ghost that gives us a sensitivity, a kindness, a patience that nothing else can give us. It is the Holy Ghost that gives us an appreciation of the tremendous value of others. Parley P. Pratt, in the most perfect description of true character development I have ever read, indicates there is no facet of human character and personality that cannot be brought into full bloom under the workings and presence of the Holy Ghost. He writes:

> An intelligent being, in the image of God, possesses every organ, attribute, sense, sympathy, affection that is possessed by God himself.
>
> But these are possessed by man, in his rudimental state, in a subordinate sense of the word. Or, in other words, these attributes are in embryo; and are to be gradually developed. They resemble a bud, a germ, which gradually develops into bloom, and then, by progress, produces the mature fruit, after its own kind.
>
> The gift of the Holy Ghost adapts itself to all these organs or attributes. It quickens all the intellectual faculties, increases, enlarges, expands and purifies all the natural passions and affections and adapts them by the gift of wisdom to their lawful use. It inspires, develops, cultivates and matures all the fine-toned sympathies, joys, tastes, kindred feelings and affections of our nature. It inspires virtue, kindness, goodness, tenderness, gentleness and charity. It develops beauty of person, form and features. It tends to health, vigor, animation and social feeling. It invigorates all the faculties of the physical and intellectual man. It strengthens and gives tone to the nerves. In short, it is, as it were, marrow to the bone, joy to the heart, light to the eyes, music to the ears, and life to the whole being. (Parley P. Pratt, *Key to the Science of Theology*, Salt Lake City: Deseret Book, 1973, pp. 100-101.)

Surely as we reflect on the role and power of the Spirit in the great missionary effort of the Church—that of bearing special witness to those who hear the gospel for the first time and of

enticing and inviting them to come into the waters of baptism—
and as we contemplate further that it is the Spirit that enables us to
gain self-control over our bodies; that it is the Spirit that gives a
remission of sins and cleanses and purifies sin-laden souls; that it
is the Spirit that distills the very nature of the Redeemer into our
beings as we live by faith; that it is the Spirit that endows faithful
believers in Christ with charity, the pure love of Christ; that it is
the Spirit that seals all ordinances according to the faithfulness of
the members so that heavenly assurances of eternal life can be
obtained while we are yet in mortality—as we reflect on all of these
and many more, surely we will exclaim "what an honor, what a
privilege, what a blessing to have the gift and power of the Holy
Ghost."

Our First Commandment

Some time ago I read a portion of a close friend's patriarchal
blessing that read as follows: "You made a covenant with the Lord
at the time of your baptism that you would live the gospel
principles and a servant of God, bearing the Holy Melchizedek
Priesthood, placed his hands upon your head and confirmed you a
member of the Church of Jesus Christ of Latter-day Saints and said
'receive the Holy Ghost.' That was a simple phrase, nothing
impressive, but it is wise counsel to you, probably the most
important admonition that you shall receive in this life." What a
beautiful thought! While we receive automatically at our confirmation the gift of the Holy Ghost we do not receive the power of the
Holy Ghost unless we seek mightily for it. Indeed, to stress the
point, the first commandment we receive when we are confirmed
members of the Church is to "receive the Holy Ghost."

Brigham Young told of an experience he had when the Prophet
Joseph Smith appeared to him many years after Joseph's death:

Joseph stepped toward me and looking very earnestly,
yet pleasantly, said: Tell the people to be humble and

faithful, and be sure to keep the spirit of the Lord and it will lead them right. Be careful and not turn away the small still voice; it will teach them what to do and where to go; it will yield the fruits of the Kingdom. Tell the brethren to keep their hearts open to conviction, so that when the Holy Ghost comes to them their hearts will be ready to receive it. They can tell the spirit of the Lord from all spirits; it will whisper peace and joy to their souls; it will take malice, hatred, strife and all evil from their hearts; and their whole desire will be to do good, bring forth righteousness and build up the Kingdom of God. Tell the brethren if they will follow the spirit of the Lord, they will go right. Be sure to tell the people to keep the spirit of the Lord; and if they will, they will find themselves just as they were organized by our Father in Heaven before they came into the world. Our Father in Heaven organized the human family, but they are all disorganized and in great confusion." (*Journal History,* February 23, 1847.)   President Wilford Woodruff shared a similar experience when he saw Brigham Young after Brigham's death:

On one occasion, I saw Brother Brigham and Brother Heber ride in a carriage ahead of the carriage in which I rode when I was on my way to attend conference and they were dressed in the most priestly robes. When we arrived at our destination, I asked President Young if he would preach to us. He said, "No, I have finished my testimony in the flesh. I shall not talk to this people anymore. But (said he) I have come to see you; I have come to watch over you, and to see what the people are doing. Then (said he) I want you to teach the people— and I want you to follow this counsel yourself—that they must labor and so live as to obtain the Holy Spirit, for without this you cannot build up the kingdom; without the spirit of God you are in danger of walking in the

128   *What it Means to Know Christ*

dark, and in danger of failing to accomplish your calling
as apostles and as elders in the church and kingdom of
God." (*JD* 21:317-318.)

Considering the profound spiritual experiences the prophets
Joseph Smith and Brigham Young enjoyed and the fact that they
grasped in such an awesome way the splendor and magnificence
of the theology of the gospel of Christ, I find it tremendously
significant that as they each visited with their successor in the
kingdom of God, their counsel and advice was simply, "Seek for
and live by the Spirit!"

When the Son of Man returns in great glory at his second
coming, the parable of the ten virgins will be fulfilled: those who
will be caught up to meet him will be those "that are wise and have
received the truth, *and have taken the Holy Spirit for their guide,* and
have not been deceived . . . [they] shall not be hewn down and cast
into the fire, but shall abide the day." (D&C 45:57; emphasis
added.)

So often in gospel discussions we hear detailed elaborations on
what the Savior really meant when he said, "Therefore I would that
ye should be perfect even as I, or your Father who is in heaven is
perfect." (3 Nephi 12:48.) Most of the elaborations imply that
perfection, in the fullest sense is an achievement for another world.
While in mortality could one consider a more worthy goal of finite
perfection than to enjoy a remission of sins and the constant
companionship of the Holy Ghost? The Lord himself promised,
"that which is of God is light; and he that receiveth light, and
continueth in God, receiveth more light; and that light groweth
brighter and brighter until the *perfect* day." (D&C 50:24.) Further,
our beloved Redeemer declared: "And if your eye be single to my
glory, your whole bodies shall be filled with light, and there shall
be no darkness in you: and that body which is filled with light
comprehendeth all things." (D&C 88:67.) What marvelous
promises, and they are predicated on and achieved by our seeking
for and obtaining the Spirit in our lives.

Living by the Spirit, then, should be our food and our drink, our desire and our determination. We should be willing to do anything and everything we have to do to successfully obtain and live by the Spirit. Brigham Young declared:

> I never cared but for one thing, and that is, simply to know that I am right before my Father in Heaven. If I am this moment, this day doing the things God requires of my hands, and precisely where my Father in Heaven wants me to be, I care no more about tomorrow than though it would never come. (*JD* 1:132.)

The Still Small Voice

It's very important to understand that in all due respect to the marvelous, spectacular manifestations of God's power to the children of men down through the ages (dividing the Red Sea, manna from heaven, etc.) and the great blessings of those manifestations, that the most common method of revelation, in fact the very spirit of revelation is the quiet whisperings of the Holy Ghost to the heart of man (D&C 8:2-3).

Elijah learned the lesson that the Lord was not in the wind, earthquakes or fire, but rather he was in the still small voice (1 Kings 19:11-12). The Nephites and Lamanites seemed to experience what the Lord had taught Elijah when, having been exposed to wind, fire and earthquake, and even having seen the descent of the resurrected Christ in their midst, that which seemed to have the greatest impact upon them was "hearing a voice that was neither harsh nor loud but a voice that did pierce them to their very center and did cause them to quake and their hearts to burn." (3 Nephi 11:3.) So it is with the Holy Ghost: Most of the knowledge we acquire from God, most of the changes that transpire are by the quiet workings of the Spirit.

Reasons We Don't Get the Spirit

Many are the reasons the Saints don't enjoy the guidance of the Spirit in their lives as they should. Obtaining the Spirit in a consistent way rests upon the broad foundation of keeping the commandments and honoring covenants made with the Lord. President Joseph Fielding Smith noted:

> We have a great many members of the Church who have never reached a manifestation through the Holy Ghost, why? Because they have not made their lives conform to the truth. That great gift comes to us only through humility, faith, and obedience. Therefore a great many members of the Church do not have that guidance. (*CN* November 4, 1961, p. 14.)

I would suggest some additional and specific things that keep us from enjoying the Spirit in the manner we should.

We Don't Ask

My experience has taught me that there are many Saints who simply are not aware that they should be seeking for the Spirit in their lives; consequently they do not seek for it. Oh how we, like the twelve disciples, should kneel down and pray for "that which they most desired; and they desired that the Holy Ghost should be given unto them." (3 Nephi 19:9.)

We Go to the Lord Only in Times of Trouble

As indicated in an earlier chapter, we need to cling to the iron rod or word of God. In a symbolic sense, we should move along the iron rod hand over hand, never removing one hand unless the other one has a solid grasp on the iron rod. Often we use the Lord and his power only when great difficulties transpire or tragedies strike; when things really get rough, we run to him with great intensity pleading for help. We ought to strive continually to enjoy his Spirit. We ought to reach for his presence, blessings and powers when things are going well, when the sun is shining, and there are no apparent storm clouds or shadows. We need to let the Lord know how much we appreciate all of our blessings while those blessings abound in rich abundance, and then when the storm clouds gather, when the Gethsemanes come, we will have the solid assurance that having sought the Lord in our prosperity, he will be with us in our trials. We will discover that every trial, indeed, every challenging experience that comes into our lives will be a stepping stone to greater heights and the very means by which we will in time become sanctified.

As indicated in the hundred and first section of the Doctrine and Covenants, verses seven and eight, the Lord chastised the Saints in Missouri for not acknowledging him in their lives when things were going well—in fact, he chided them for turning to him only when great difficulties came upon them. Perhaps you remember that at the time this revelation was given, the Saints had been driven from Jackson County because of envying and strife (verse 5). In fact, they had been told that they needed to be tested and tried even as Abraham (verse 4). For our purposes, let's change the plural pronoun in verses seven and eight to the singular, and perhaps in doing so, we will appreciate more how desperately we need to cling to the Lord at all times.

> You were slow to hearken unto the voice of the Lord your God; therefore, the Lord your God is slow to hearken unto your prayers, to answer them in the day of your trouble. In the day of your peace you esteemed lightly my counsel; but in the day of your trouble, of necessity you feel after me.

I'm completely convinced that if we sense our dependency on the Lord and seek mightily for the Spirit that through sunshine and darkness, we will have the comforter to be with us.

We Are Not Decisive

So many times as we seek for the mind and will of the Lord in our lives, we seriously limit our ability to obtain the Lord's direction because we are not decisive enough—that is, we don't think through our problems, weigh carefully the various options, select the one we think is right, and then seek in prayer for a confirmation (D&C 9:8). The Lord expects us to do our homework, to make a choice, to step out, as it were, to the edge of light and to give him a tangible decision that he can work with in our behalf. Too often we are afraid to make the decisions because we don't know what to decide, and it becomes more difficult when despite our earnest prayers, we seemingly receive no explicit direction. But if we are willing to make a decision on the basis of our best judgment, he will stand by us in the decision we make. Brigham illustrates this principle:

> If I do not know the will of the Father, and what he requires of me in a certain transaction, if I ask him to give me wisdom concerning any requirement in life, or in regard to my own course or that of my friends, my family, my children, or those that I preside over and get no answer from him and then do the very best that my judgment will teach me, he is bound to own and honor that transaction, and he will do so to all intents and purposes. (*JD* 3:205.)

I'll not forget the time a young lady came into my office with an unusually difficult problem. As I listened closely to the details she shared with me, I felt she really needed the help of the Brethren. I told her a General Authority was coming the next day as a devotional speaker and that perhaps she could slip him a note indicating her problem and asking for his advice. She accepted my suggestion and received two days later a letter from the General Authority which read, in effect, "Dear Sister, thank you for your note and I'm most sympathetic with the challenge you have in making the correct decision. May I suggest you think through various alternatives very carefully, present the one you think is the best to the Lord, ask him if it is correct . . ."

The Lord desperately wants you and me to be decisive, to

present our decisions to him so we can learn to understand the whisperings of the Spirit in response to the decisions we make.

We Expect Too Much Too Soon

Obtaining the companionship of the Spirit on a regular basis isn't something that comes at the snap of a finger, simply from desiring it. One discovers quickly that it takes time and a great deal of patience to harmonize one's desires with those of the Lord, to be willing to give one's free agency completely to Christ, to discipline the thoughts and intents of the heart and the words spoken by the tongue. One must be careful of the friends that one chooses and the recreation one engages in. Seeking mightily for the blessings and the directions of the Master can be risky—one can't seek for and grow in the spirit of revelation but what it is an open invitation to be tempted of the adversary—it appears that the degree to which God reveals himself to man is the degree to which he allows Satan to tempt us. We can't genuinely claim a revelation or endowment of power is truly ours until Satan tries to take it from us and we successfully resist his every effort.

To grow in the spirit of revelation takes time and patience and perseverence, but if we keep our faces turned heavenward and keep struggling even though our progress often seems so slow, in time we will reach our goal and enjoy on a regular basis the companionship of the Holy Ghost.

Perhaps the following analogy will be helpful in emphasizing the tremendous importance of having great patience as we try to grow in our ability to live by the Spirit.

I had three brothers who served in the armed forces; one as a pilot in the Air Force, and two who were paratroopers in the army. Much to my delight as a young teenager, my Air Force brother frequently brought Air Force fighter planes home. What a thrill it was to have him come over the farm house literally lower than the trees in a P—38 lightning fighter or a P—51 mustang fighter and put on an airshow just for the family! Over a period of several years and because of recurring visits on his part, I and others in the family were given many a thrilling ride—some of the time a little more thrilling than we wanted! At the same time I developed a real desire myself to learn to fly a plane. One spring, due to the generosity of another brother, arrangements were made for me to receive flying lessons at the local airport.

The day I went out to have my first lesson was absolutely beautiful—a few fluffy clouds were in the sky, there was no wind, and it was just perfect for flying. Hoping we would quickly get in the plane and take off, I was very disappointed that the instructor insisted on taking up a lot of valuable time talking about the basic structure and important parts of the airplane—I felt I was already familiar with the structure and parts. It seemed so ridiculous to walk around the plane so many times while he went on and on about things that seemed totally irrelevent—I wanted to fly! I didn't want to know how to make an airplane! It took all the patience I could muster to keep from blurting out, "Hey, look, when it comes to airplanes, I've been around and up in dozens of them. I already know the things you're telling me. Let's get in the plane and up in the air." Finally, we climbed aboard, I in the front cockpit and he right behind me. The plane had a tail wheel instead of a nose wheel so the nose was much higher than the tail, pointing the plane at an angle that made it impossible for the pilot to see the runway directly ahead. My instructor indicated the first thing I was to learn was how to taxi down the runway going from one side to the other so I would be able to see if there were other aircraft on the runway. That sounded simple enough. The runway looked like it was at least 60 feet wide, the controls seemed easy enough to handle, I was a fair athlete with what I thought was reasonably good muscular coordination, and I just knew that taxiing back and forth per instruction would be a cinch. After receiving what I thought were more than adequate instructions, the engine was started, the brake was released, and we started down the runway. Immediately, I was absolutely astounded at how sensitive the controls were! Having been told to zigzag back and forth across the runway, I had barely begun to zig the runway when I was all the way across, and before I could zag I had run off and was making tracks in the sagebrush and grass. The instructor yelled at me to get back on the runway which I quickly did, but only momentarily because I over-corrected and was now off on the other side! The instructor got pretty excited—so excited that I thought he was going to be the first instructor who bailed out of a plane before it had even taken off!

I was so frustrated, irritated, embarrassed, and disappointed at how hard it was to properly handle the controls that I wanted to tell the instructor to stop what I thought was a very temperamental plane and I would immediately cease my flying lessons for good. However, he was patient and I was somewhat determined; consequently, I eventually got so I could handle the controls just right, taxiing smoothly while staying all the time on the runway. After practicing a few more times, the big moment finally arrived—we took off and oh, what a thrill to my young heart to be at the controls of the plane, to lift off the ground, to gain adequate altitude, and then to fly around the valley. It was more than worth all the frustration of achieving adequate control.

So it is with trying to live by the Spirit. It is frustrating to try to arrive at a point where we can handle and control our mind, our tongue, our desires and passions so that the sensitive, delicate promptings of the Spirit can enable us to thread our way through the subtle, sensuality of our day and the clouds of intellectual sophistry which are so prevalent on every side. It takes time and patience to learn to discern the promptings of the Spirit, to learn the boundaries, rules, and regulations for receiving personal revelation. It can be discouraging, but in seeking to live by the Spirit, we are attempting to do the single most important and challenging thing on earth and we should anticipate a tremendous soul-stretching experience. We must realize that having the Spirit is more than worth the struggle it takes to obtain it.

Further, it is so important to realize that if our hearts are pure and we genuinely desire righteousness and we diligently keep the commandments, honor the prophets and pray mightily, the Lord's power, strength and direction will be ours. We may not enjoy the visions, the dreams, and the open revelations that we desire as soon as we would like them, but we will, without qualification, have peace, and in that peace the sweet assurance that if we endure in righteousness, ultimately everything will be ours.

To be patient in seeking for the Spirit is to be patient in well-doing (D&C 64:33), and there are few if any experiences that will fashion a crown of righteousness for us to inherit ultimately than persisting mightily in seeking "to be a greater follower of right-eousness, and to possess a greater knowledge." (Abraham 1:2.)

The following personal experiences are shared to help illustrate the challenge it is to obtain the guidance of the Spirit; that it is often one thing to know the Lord is with you and another thing to discern exactly what he is telling you; that often some of the most important decisions we make stem from an almost imperceptible whisper of the Spirit. I know, however, if we will persist and not get discouraged, we will grow in the spirit of revelation.

Being Strengthened for Sorrow

To my recollection, the first encounter I had with the Spirit (although I didn't understand what was happening) was on February 12, 1939. I was nine years old. My closest childhood friend and I were walking through the neighborhood, chewing gum and chatting as friends do. It had rained the night before, leaving many puddles on the unpaved road. We crossed an alley and walked by an open garage. As I walked past the garage I glanced in, noticing the garage was empty; but right at that moment, there flooded over me a powerful feeling—I'll never forget it. The feeling imprinted every detail of the moment into my mind. I didn't know what it meant or what was happening, but I did know that the feeling was real and very unique, and that something very important was being made known to me.

In time we ended up at my friend's house, went upstairs, and were somehow playing in his bedroom. I heard the phone ring downstairs and, somehow, immediately knew it was for me and that my mother had died. Before my friend's sister finished answering the phone I had grabbed my coat, run downstairs, and was on my way home. As I hurried home to meet my bereaved father and brothers and sisters, I felt a comfort that I will never forget—a comfort that was such a blessing that day and in the months to come.

Go To School

Most of the whisperings of the Spirit that have changed my life in the most dramatic way didn't seem that consequential at the time. For example, most of my growing up years were spent on a farm and I grew to love working in the fields. Even before the completion of high school, I was determined to make farming my life's vocation. Following high school, I attended a year of college at Logan, after which I served my mission. I remember visiting with elders on different occasions and when the subject of future plans would come up, I emphasized that my college days were over and that after my mission I would return to the farm, get married, and live happily thereafter. Although I enjoyed my experience at Logan, I had no desire or inclination whatsoever to return to college.

I returned from my mission at Christmas time, started preparing the tractor and machinery for the coming spring and really looked forward to settling down to a life of agriculture. It was great to get back into the swing of farming and when spring came I was delighted to put my hand to the plow, so to speak, again very convinced that that was where it would remain. However, much to my surprise, I found myself very restless after just a few months of farming. It was hard to pin down my feelings—I enjoyed what I was doing and yet there was a vague feeling of discontent.

One morning I was walking over to the south end of the farm to change the water. I had a shovel over my shoulder and wasn't really thinking of anything in particular when quite unexpectedly (to put it mildly), there came into my mind and heart the idea that I should return to college that fall, and that it should be to BYU. The idea came so forcefully and caught me so totally off guard that I flipped the shovel off my shoulder, quickly turned and ran all the way back to the farmhouse and excitedly announced to my dad and stepmother that I knew, without question, that I should return to college. Although I didn't know what I should study, I knew I should be in school, and that one idea changed the entire course of my life. Little did I dream that because of that powerful intimation of the Spirit I would be willing to stick with my education until I finally obtained all three degrees.

After my wife and I were married, the children came with clock-like regularity, and of necessity I had to teach constantly to survive economically, there were many moments when I seriously questioned the validity of what I was attempting to do. But always at the moment of greatest discouragement, there would come into my mind that precious experience of walking along a dirt road, and learning so fully that the most important thing for me to do then was to return to college. With that remembrance, renewed determination would come that enabled me, finally, to reach my goals.

It's Important Where You Ski

Have you ever ignored the distinct promptings of the Spirit and then suffered from missing an opportunity or a blessing? Let me share with you an experience when that happened to me.

I was particularly close to my brother who was just older than I. We spent long hours together working in the fields, milking the cows, double dating, playing on the same football team for a year, and other things. Just prior to my mission, he married his childhood sweetheart and I was his best man. We corresponded

regularly while I was in the mission field and in that correspond-
ence I learned that he and his wife were very active in a little
branch in Oregon. It was at that point in his life that he obtained a
personal testimony of the divinity of the restoration, which was a
source of great delight to me.

After returning from my mission, what a special thrill it was to
have my brother and his family come home for Christmas. I'll not
forget how excited I was to see him and embrace him again. I was
so anxious to share with him the joys of missionary work, but his
excitement for his new-found testimony and his desire to share it
with me precluded my getting much said. Several days later we
decided to take a skiing trip to Sun Valley, Idaho. I had four friends
who were home recently from their missions and/or the armed
forces, and I invited them to come and join us.

After arriving in Sun Valley, we commenced skiing on Dollar
Mountain, which is a beginner's mountain and isn't terribly
challenging; so it wasn't too surprising when my four close friends
and I decided it would be more exciting to go over to Baldy
Mountain to finish out the day of skiing. After we made the
decision, I skied over to where my brother was and asked him if he
would like to go over to Baldy with us. He declined the invitation
by saying he wasn't sure if he was ready to tackle the more difficult
slopes of Mount Baldy, but he encouraged me to go with my
friends if I so desired.

At that moment it seemed that the Spirit said quietly but firmly,
"George, stay and ski with your brother. Spend the day with him
and let your friends go on over to Baldy." I resisted strongly the
prompting with the retort, "Listen, what difference does it make
where I ski? My goodness, I've been on a mission for two years and
you hounded me constantly there. Can't I have one day of skiing
without you telling me where I should ski? Not only that, what
difference could it possibly make where I ski?"

I continued to feel that I shouldn't go with my friends, but I went
anyway. While riding on the ski bus from Dollar Mountain to
Baldy I felt terrible—it seemed that the Spirit was really grieved

with me for not responding to his promptings. I spent the remainder of the day skiing with my friends, but it wasn't particularly enjoyable. At the end of the day we all piled in the car and returned home. Early the next morning my brother, his wife, and their new son left for Oregon.

The next time I saw my beloved brother was six months later. He was lying in a hospital bed in Oregon stricken with the advanced stages of a terrible cancer. As I quietly stepped into his hospital room and saw him lying there so sick and weak that he could hardly acknowledge me, there came into my mind the scene that transpired on Dollar Mountain. I then realized that the Lord, who knows all things, had tried to tell me on Dollar Mountain; "Look, this is the last day you'll be with your brother. Being with your friends is important, but not nearly as important as being with your brother," but I wouldn't listen. How marvelous it would have been to have spent that last day with my brother, skiing with him, pausing and chatting with him, and sharing ideas about the gospel.

Misreading the Spirit

That summer when my brother was stricken with cancer and eight weeks later, died, I learned one of the hardest lessons on personal revelation that I have ever learned. When I first was told that Warren had cancer, I immediately went into a pattern of fasting and prayer. I pled night and day that the Lord would spare his life—it seemed to me he had every reason to live. He had finally finished his schooling, he had a good job, he had just been blessed with a beautiful son, he and his wife were happily married, and he and his wife were preparing to go to the temple to be sealed that fall.

As I wrestled in mighty prayer, fasting each week, there came a great peace into my heart. The calm feeling was one of such intensity that I felt for sure that Warren would be healed. I continued to fast and pray and by the time three weeks had elapsed, I was completely convinced that he would not die and that all would be well. I announced to his wife that I knew he would soon be healed. I announced it to the family and relatives. I announced it boldly and strongly. I wrote it in letters. I was so sure.

Eight weeks after Warren knew he had cancer, he passed away. I was devastated. It was so hard to understand. Why had I failed to recognize what the Lord was telling me? There was absolutely no question that he had spoken peace to my heart and how could I have peace unless he were to live?.

The day of the funeral, I and an older brother who was inactive in the Church were in the bathroom preparing for the services. My heart was already so heavy I could hardly bear it when the casual conversation ended abruptly and my brother, whom I love dearly, became critical of me and my foolish faith. "Surely," he said, "the wind has been knocked out of you for being so unwise as to promise everyone our brother would live." He really reprimanded me both for my belief and my having made such promises.

Obviously, the words cut deeply—what could I say? How could I defend myself, and for that matter, the concept of healing by faith? After my brother finished, I walked up the stairs and outside. It was a beautiful June day. As I glanced upward, some feelings of rebelliousness and resentment surfaced in my mind and the thought formulated, "Heavenly Father, if you think I will ever try again to understand your mind and your will through the Spirit, you're wrong!" I didn't say it, but I would be less than honest in not admitting that I was deeply hurt, terribly embarrassed, and very confused.

Yet, while sitting in the chapel during the proceedings of the funeral, I felt peace come into my heart. I quickly and vividly recalled the many times the whisperings of the Spirit, the revelations of the Holy Ghost, had come so unmistakably into my heart. I recalled the sureness and intensity of when I learned Jesus is the Christ, that Joseph Smith is a prophet, and that the Book of

Mormon is true. Many beautiful memories of the workings of the Spirit at other times in my life flooded into my mind and heart. Indeed, peace came, and with that peace the thought distilled deeply into my being, "It is one thing to know that my Spirit is upon you, but it is another thing to discern correctly what I am trying to reveal to you." I learned a great deal from that entire experience. I vowed I would try harder to discern the workings of the Spirit.

There is No Witness Until . . .

Another challenge that presents itself in trying to live by the Spirit is this: Some of the time the Lord seems to insist that we make a decision and implement that decision before we get a total confirmation that the decision is correct. It is an interesting but somewhat nerve-wracking principle.

One summer day my father and I were irrigating some sugar beets and chatting back and forth. I remember leaning on my shovel and listening intently as he informed me that if I was interested in farming for a livelihood, he would be pleased to will everything to me, which at the time would have been a fairly sizable inheritance. He indicated, however, that if I weren't interested in agriculture as a life-long vocation, he would make arrangements to have everything divided equally among all members of the family. I responded by telling him I appreciated his offer and that I would keep it in mind and see how things developed in the next several years.

In time I served my mission and then commenced the pattern of alternating between going to school and farming. After three years, I married. My sweetheart and I hoped we could finish school but because of Dad's failing health, we returned to the farm for what we thought would be "one season"; however, we ended up staying there for five years. Shortly after arriving back on the farm, I received an invitation to teach full-time seminary, which I gladly accepted. Now, because of both farming and teaching, I found it extremely difficult to finish my Bachelor's degree.

One spring morning the telephone rang. It was an administrator in the Church Educational System. He said, "Brother Pace, we are making part-time teaching assignments in the valley, here [Provo] for teachers who want to finish their degrees. Would you be interested in accepting one of those assignments?"

I immediately began to tell him all the reasons why it would be very difficult to drop everything and return to school. He said he appreciated the fact that it would be a challenge, but he didn't call to hear all of that—he simply wanted to know if I wanted to do it. He said, "You make the decision! I'll call back tomorrow morning at 10:00 a.m. to find out what it is. Goodbye!"

Both my wife and I felt it was an awfully important decision—I remember how we were both stunned that we had to make the decision before 10:00 a.m. the next day! I felt that if I ever left the farm to go back to school full time, we would never return. It was just a feeling, but nevertheless it was strong and caused me some concern. We immediately prayed with all of our hearts, together and separately, about what we should do. That night, we bundled our three little girls up, pajamas and all, and hurried up the hill where the folks lived, told them our plight, and asked them what they thought we should do. I remember Dad saying, "I can't make your decision for you, but I will tell you one thing for sure— whatever you decide to do, we will support you one hundred percent." I wanted to say, "Well thanks, Dad, but won't you make our decision for us?" I had a lot of weaknesses, but one that gave me perhaps the most difficulty was that of indecisiveness. The Lord knew I desperately needed to be placed in a position where the decision had to be made and had to be made now.

After continued discussions and struggling in prayer, we decided we should return to school. I took the decision to the Lord and expected either an immediate confirmation or a stupor of thought—I didn't receive either! I felt more of a 50/50 feeling. I returned in prayer and pled with the Lord for a clear-cut answer.

Still, there was no tipping of the scales. I reminded the Lord that this was one of the most important decisions of my life—still no stronger feeling one way or the other. The following morning I indicated to the Lord that I absolutely had to know before 10:00 a.m., but that didn't seem to help at all. Finally, the phone rang at the appointed hour. I boldly answered the expected query with, "Yes, yes, I'm going to come back and finish my degree!" Even as I voiced my decision and showed (finally) some real decisiveness, I found myself glancing upward and thinking in my mind, "Now, Lord, you know without question that I'm serious about my decision. Would you be kind enough to give me a confirmation before I hang up the phone?" But still I couldn't discern even a slight ripple in my feelings.

All of this occurred early in the spring. We weren't actually going to leave until fall, so I continued to strive in every way I knew how to obtain the coveted confirmation. Again, I felt that this was a crucial decision, one that would affect my entire life, my family, and my loved ones. Throughout the following months I kept struggling for the confirmation, but no confirmation came.

Finally, the big day arrived. We backed a two-ton farm truck up to the little house where we had spent the first five years of our married life. Just the memories of what had occurred during those most important years made the thought of leaving unbelievably hard, let alone knowing that the move would terminate an unusually close association with my father. We started loading the furniture and even as I carried out a chair or a table, in my heart I was again telling the Lord that I had been and I was decisive, I was carrying out what I felt I should do and said I would do—couldn't I please, now, before actually leaving, know without question that my decision was correct? But still the answer was neither yes nor no. Although Dad was quite severly hampered with arthritis and it was most difficult for him to walk, let alone carry things, he cheerfully assisted us all he could. Still, it was easy to tell it was extremely difficult for him to have us leave.

After the truck was loaded, with a heavy heart I put a little padlock on the door of the house, kissed my dad and stepmother goodbye, and got in the truck. We drove out of the lane, across the creek that ran not far from the house, and up onto US 30, heading the truck toward Utah. All the while my heart strings were being pulled harder than at any previous time in my life. The truck had four gears ahead, and with the heavy load, it took some time to pick up enough speed, finally, to get it shifted into the fourth gear. After that last shift, with my foot firmly planted on the accelerator, wondering if I would emotionally survive the feelings that were coming, it happened—the confirmation came! And what a confirmation! The refulgence of the Spirit came with such intensity that if there was ever a perfect knowledge of anything, surely this was it! The peace, the bouyancy, the tingling excitement—I thought I would be lifted right off the seat! I felt like I had a date with destiny and I knew, I knew, I knew that the decision was correct, acceptable to the Lord, and that he was pleased.

I cried out in my heart, "Oh Lord, why, why did you wait so long to give me my confirmation? Why didn't you give it to me months ago?" There came into my mind with some force the following words: "Ye receive no witness until after the trial of your faith." (Ether 12:6.)

It was true, as I had suspected, that having left the farm, I never returned except for periodic visits. The decision to return to school terminated five choice years of Seminary, but opened the door to the Institute program, and then in time to an opportunity to serve at the Church university and to enjoy the many privileges and opportunities that came from such positions.

Don't Count the Cost

As we are exposed to more and more experiences of life within the setting of the Church and kingdom of God, we become quite mindful that the way we determine whether or not we should do a particular thing isn't by asking first whether or not we can afford to do it, but rather by finding out what the Lord would have us do and then bend every effort to do it. That's a challenging lesson to learn, but one that continually makes its appearance as we try to live by faith. One experience that taught me a great lesson in this area and helped me appreciate the blessing of having the companionship of the Spirit is the following.

My wife was raised in Portland, Oregon, a city girl through and through and not acquainted at all with the ways of the farmer. It is ironic that a year before we met and married, while traveling through Idaho on her way to BYU, she had observed to friends in the car, "I can't imagine living in one of those tiny houses out in the middle of nowhere!" Almost before she realized what was happening, she found herself plunked in one of those little farm houses—out in the middle of nowhere!

Although I convinced her quite often to join me in the barn while I was milking the cows, she never became accustomed to the smell and only rarely would she actually consent to touch a cow; she wondered why it was necessary to milk cows twice a day— what a waste of time and effort, she would say—why not just milk them at noon and let it go at that? Irrigating was another puzzlement to her. It seemed absurd to her to have to irrigate every ten days—why not really flood the place and let that last for a month? It was hard for her to realize that during the summer months, which ordinarily are vacation time, it was next to impossible to make a trip to Portland to see her parents and family. The demands of milking night and morning, constantly irrigating, cultivating, and so forth, plus being on a limited budget, all joined in making even a three or four day trip home to visit her folks a herculean effort. However, each summer we would make the trip in spite of the great difficulty. I might add that the fact that her folks had a motor boat and lived right on the banks of the Willamette River, which facilitated some great water-skiing, was somewhat of an enticement for the annual trip in spite of the challenge.

This particular year, early in the summer, I determined that there was simply no way we could make the trip. We were running an additional farm along with ours, the work load was piling up, and we were broke. Realizing that on several occasions in previous years I had said, "We cannot and will not make the trip!" and then a few days later had given in and changed my mind, I knew that I would have to be firm in announcing my decision. I would have to make the announcement to her with a patriarchal note of finality in my voice. In fact, my wife hd already bestowed the dubious title "tower of jelly" upon me, because there were many times I would boldly announce new plans, programs and policies that I just knew would enable the family to be translated in six months, and then I'd have to back down after trying it for only three days! Somehow, my firm patriarchal announcements had a tendency to disintegrate whenever I would see even the beginning of a tear form in the eye of my wife, or when one of my daughters would slip their arms around me and tell me what a great guy I was!

Well, after getting myself fully prepared, I marched into the kitchen, stood in front of my Sweetie and announced with great solemnity that we would not be going to Portland that summer. I then turned and hurried out of the house hoping to get out fast enough not to hear her laughing. Several weeks later I was walking out across an alfalfa field, not thinking of anything in particular, when clearly and so powerfully the spirit seemed to announce to my heart, "George, I want you to tell your wife to prepare herself and the little girls to go to Portland tomorrow!" I thought I would die! I remember glancing up and mentally saying, "Do you know with what finality I told my wife we would not go to Portland?" But the feeling persisted so strongly that I spun around, hurried back to the house, marched in, stood in front of Sweetie and quickly said, "Please get yourself and the children ready for a trip. We are going to Portland in the morning!" I hurried out, hoping I wouldn't hear her laughing, but—I wasn't halfway out the door when her laughter reached my ears.

The following morning we left for Portland, arriving in the early evening. As indicated earlier, on previous trips I was able to do a lot of water-skiing, and we had also done some sightseeing on occasion. This time, though, we all just stayed in the house and talked and talked. After two days I began to get quite nervous and really wondered why there had seemed to be such an urgency to come. I announced to the family that we would leave early the next morning. After breakfast and family prayer the next day, I loaded the baggage and the three little girls, and then started the car and waited impatiently for Diane to come out and get in the car. Several minutes later she came out with her parents, walking particularly close to her father. As she came to the right side of the car, she and her father slipped their arms around one another and shared deeply their feelings for one another. As I sat and watched and listened, I thought, "What a beautiful experience. What a great father-daughter relationship they have. How dearly they love one another." At that moment a feeling came into my heart indicating that that was the reason the trip was made. I felt at peace and not so anxious about things. I then knew that that was the reason why we had come to Portland.

We then returned to Idaho and carried on with the many things that needed to be done. One week later, we received a long-distance call—it was Diane's mother. She informed us that Ralph, Diane's father, had passed away very suddenly from a fairly routine operation. Immediately, there came into my mind with great clarity the experience just weeks before of walking across the alfalfa field and the Lord making known to me that I should take my wife home to see her father one last time. It didn't matter that we couldn't afford it, it didn't matter that there was too much work to do. How grateful I was that the Lord in his loving kindness prompted me to make that significant trip.

Fulfilling the divine purposes of our membership in the Church is inextricably tied to seeking for and obtaining the guidance and direction of the Holy Spirit. It is through the workings of the Spirit that we develop a close, personal relationship with the Savior. One cannot be moved upon by the Spirit in giving a talk but what he senses the personal presence of the Lord. One cannot receive a confirmation of an important decision but what he senses Christ is his friend. That man or woman who is most alive to the reality of God and Christ and the infinite privilege of earth life is that man or woman who is filled with the Holy Spirit.

Don't let a day go by but what you plead with all the faith you possess that you might have the constant guidance and com panionship of the Holy Ghost. If you will seek and seek diligently, you will come to know without question that Jesus Christ is your sole source of the light, life and love you need to become totally like him.

Chapter 7

To Know The Lord Is To Know That He Is A God Of Power And That By And Through Him We Can Fulfill All His Commandments

One of the crops we raised on our farm in Idaho that seemed to require more work than any other was the sugar beet crop. Thinning the beets was a backbreaking job, for it had to be done with a short-handled hoe. Throughout the summer, the weeds continually had to be hoed. In the fall, the beets had to be dug one row at a time and the tops cut off, often in the rain and snow. Finally, they were hauled to the sugar beet dump in wagons pulled by teams of horses. The memories of planting, raising, and harvesting sugar beets have left such indelible impressions on my mind that whenever I get discouraged with teaching, I just reminisce for a while about my experiences with sugar beets and I loose all discouragement!

There was one experience related to harvesting sugar beets that has left a bright spot in my memory and from which I learned an important lesson. After my brothers and I would top several rows of beets by hand, my father would drive the wagon, pulled by a team of horses, between the rows and we would load the wagon by hand with five to seven tons of beets. Because it was not uncommon for us to harvest in rain and snow, it frequently became very difficult for the horses to pull the loaded wagon out of the wet, muddy fields. Often Dad would let me try my skill at driving the team of horses under those difficult circumstances, and what a sense of satisfaction and feeling of power was mine as a thirteen-year-old when I was able to successfully accomplish the feat of getting the loaded wagon out of the muddy field. Many times I would compliment myself, thinking, "Wow, George, look what you're doing! You are responsible for seeing that seven tons of beets are being pulled out of the field!" However, it was quite a humbling thought one day to realize *that the power that was holding the reins was not the same power that was pulling the load!*

So it is with us. I believe that one of the most important lessons for all of us to learn is that it is by the Lord's power and only by His power that we are able to accomplish all that the Lord wants us to do. It is true that we might possess administrative ability, we might enjoy remarkable success in the field of business or other areas, we might have professional training and be highly skilled—we might, as it were, hold the reins in responsible callings in the kingdom; but if the wagon is to be pulled successfully, if we are to be enabled to do all the Lord would have us do, it will be by the Lord's power and not our own. It is a sobering thought to realize that it is our Lord and Savior who points out the path to eternal life to us, who gives us a desire and enables us to get on the path, and who encourages us to walk the path and to journey successfully all the way to Him! If we want what we do in righteousness consecrated to the welfare of our souls, if we want to be successful in our labors in the kingdom to bring people to the Father through Christ, we absolutely must look to the Savior and obtain his power or all of our labors will be in vain.

Probably one of the greatest themes in the first book of the Book of Mormon is how Jehovah enabled Lehi and his colony to successfully escape destruction in Jerusalem and arrive safely in the promised land. Lehi was given a remarkable vision of the impending doom coming upon Jerusalem. After Nephi and his brothers had exhausted every other means to obtain the brass plates, Laban was miraculously delivered into Nephi's hands and the plates were obtained. The colony received the Liahona to guide them through the desert, without which they never could have found their way. Their meat was made sweet by the Lord so that fire, which would have attracted roving bandits, would not be necessary to cook the meat. At a time of crisis, Nephi was able to make a bow of sufficient quality to shoot wild animals for desperately needed food. Laman and Lemuel were overpowered by God several times to the preserving of Nephi's life. The women were made strong like unto the men so they could carry their burdens through the desert. Nephi was able to construct a ship designed by the Lord, and the colony was preserved upon the deep and enabled to land safely on the shores of the promised land, all of which was accomplished because the Lord manifested his marvelous power.

In all of these experiences, the Lord wanted Nephi to know "that I, the Lord, am God; and that I, the Lord, did deliver you from destruction; yea, that I did bring you out of the land of Jerusalem." (Nephi 17:14; emphasis added). Is it any wonder Nephi declared with great faith, "Oh Lord, I have trusted in thee, and I will trust in thee forever. I will not put my trust in the arm of flesh; for I know that cursed is he that putteth his trust in the arm of flesh. Yea, cursed is he that putteth his trust in man or maketh flesh his arm." (2 Nephi 4:34)

I don't think there is a better example, aside from the Lord himself, of a man who caught more fully the role God's power plays in our successes and who expressed more beautifully his appreciation for the Lord's help than Ammon, one of the missionary sons of Mosiah. His success as a missionary was phenomenal. He brought literally thousands of souls to Christ. He displayed an ability to relate to kings and servants in a manner that quickly won their confidence and trust. He taught the gospel in a way that capitalized on the limited spiritual understanding of the Lamanites. In the fullest sense of the word, he was a servant's servant, anxious to do anything and everything he could to show forth the Savior's power to his fellow servants (Alma 17:29). The power of God rested upon Ammon and allowed him to accomplish things that were so marvelous that Lamoni was convinced that Ammon was God himself, or the "great spirit." (Alma 18:11)

After their missions were over, Ammon and his brothers began to share their experiences. Ammon came on strong in his recounting of his great successes and even though he ended his brief report by saying, "Let us sing to his praise, yea, let us give thanks to his holy name, for he doth work righteousness forever," (Alma 26:8), Aaron rebuked his brother and accused him of boasting. But Ammon seems even more forceful as he gives credit where credit is due:

> I do not boast in my own strength, nor in my wisdom; but behold, my joy is full, yea, my heart is brim with joy, and I will rejoice in my God. Yea, I know that I am nothing; as to my strength I am weak; therefore I will not boast of myself, but I will boast of my God, for in his strength I can do all things; yea, behold, many mighty miracles we have wrought in this land, for which we will praise his name forever. . . . Therefore, let us glory, yea, we will glory in the Lord; yea, we will rejoice, for our joy is full; yea, we will praise our God forever. Behold, who can glory too much in the Lord? Yea, who can say too much of his great power, and of his mercy, and of his long-suffering towards the children of men? Behold, I say unto you, I cannot say the smallest part which I feel. (Alma 26:11-12, 16.)

Oh how we, like Ammon, should be most anxious to show forth the mighty works of God. How anxious we should be to bear testimony that the Lord will watch over us and bless us and enable us to accomplish great things through his power.

The prophet Moroni sums up in a remarkable way the promises and blessings that are available to those who really come to know Christ, and he leaves no question that the man of Christ or the woman of Christ will acknowledge fully that their achievements in righteousness are because of the Savior's endowment of power: "And again, if ye by the grace of God are perfect in Christ, *and deny not his power*, then are ye sanctified in Christ by the grace of God." (Moroni 10:32; emphasis added.)

How important it is not to take credit to ourselves. Probably one of the greatest tragedies in every age of enlightenment is the tendency of men and women to arrogate to themselves the credit for the things they have achieved. This tendency extends to every phase of human endeavor. Brigham Young said, "Every discovery in science and art, that is really true and useful to mankind, has been given by direct revelation from God though but few acknowledge it." (*JD* 9:369.) Joseph Fielding Smith confirmed the idea when he said:

> We see a man with extraordinary gifts, or with great intelligence, and he is instrumental in developing some great principle. He and the world ascribe genius and wisdom to himself. He attributes his success to his own energies, labor and mental capacity. He does not acknowledge the hand of the Lord in anything connected with his success, but ignores him altogether and takes the honor to himself. This will apply to almost all the world. In all the great modern discoveries in science, in the arts, in mechanics, and in all the material advancement of the age, the world says, "we have done it." The individual says, "I have done it," and he gives no honor or credit to the Lord. (*CR* October 1969, p. 110.)

We as members of the Church should be mindful that all due respect to the abilities and capacities of thousands of Saints in this last dispensation, no individual or set of individuals are responsible for the great work that has been done in the restored kingdom. That work has been done because the Savior poured out his Spirit and power upon his people. Had he not done so, the work would have been impossible. I love the following statement of President Joseph Fielding Smith, who explains in a powerful way our dependency on the Savior:

> Remember that it is the gift of God to man, that it is his power and his guiding influence that have accomplished what we see has been accomplished. It has not been done by the wisdom of men. They are instruments in the Lord's hands in accomplishing his purposes, and we should not deny that they are such; we should honor them. But when we undertake to give them the honor for accomplishing this work, and take the honor from the Lord, who qualified the men to do the work, we are doing an injustice to our Heavenly Father. (Joseph Fielding Smith, CR October 1968, p. 124.)

The Lord himself said, "In nothing doth man offend God, or against none is his wrath kindled, *save those who confess not his hand in all things,* and obey not his commandments." (D&C 59:21; emphasis added.)

God is a God of Miracles

One can't study the scriptures without recognizing that where there is faith, there are miracles. To the believers, miracles are marvelous confirmations of one's faith and devotion to the Lord. To the unbelievers, they are simply signs that have a tendency to condemn.

We are invited by the Lord to believe in his miraculous power, to realize that all things are possible to him. We need to recognize that especially between now and the second coming, the Saints need to acquire a much greater faith because the only way to survive the economic upheavals, the great persecution and the calamities that will be poured out is through the miraculous power of the Lord.

It has always been difficult for people to believe in the "miraculous." Laman and Lemuel just couldn't accept the idea that the Lord was more powerful than Laban and his soldiers (1 Nephi 3:31). It was so hard for Sarah to believe she could conceive a child at her old age that she laughed out loud (Gensis 18:12). Thousands of Nephites and Lamanites were so stunned when Samuel the Lamanite's prediction of the day, night, and day as one day was fulfilled that they fell to the earth as if they were dead. In our day, the biblical account of a universal flood, of the earth dividing in the days of Peleg, of the faithful Saints ultimately seeing eye to eye politically, economically and socially—all of these things are simply too much for some Saints to believe.

The true test the Saints face, then, is not whether they believe the Church is true, but whether they will so live their lives that they will come to know that there isn't anything God will ask them to do but what they can obtain his power to do it.

I grew up with a heavy emphasis on the idea that "God helps those who help themselves," that we must use wisdom in all things, that we need to be very realistic and practical. But with this outlook, somehow the idea of miracles—of God's actual intervention in my life—was only a minor part of my faith in Christ. However, in time, the challenges I faced became so great that the rational, practical approach simply wasn't sufficient and I knew that unless I sought for and obtained his marvelous power, unless miracles were performed, there was no way I could achieve what the Lord wanted me to do.

I believe all of us will come to a time in our lives when we realize we cannot accomplish all we were sent here to do unless we obtain his marvelous power. If we will seek his power, we will come to understand by personal experience that just as the Lord sent quails into the camps of the Israelites (Numbers 11), he can miraculously provide for our every need. We will become aware that there are many forms of modern-day manna as the Lord performs miracles that reach into every phase of our lives, making bare his arms mightily in our emotional, physical, intellectual, and financial needs as he does our spiritual needs.

Obtaining a Sense of Destiny

Something deeply motivating happens when the Spirit of the Lord burns into our souls the great truth that in the eyes of God each one of us is infinitely important! That we really matter! That each one of us can make a great deal of difference in the unfolding drama of God's plan of redemption! I believe that long before any of us receive the promise of eternal life and perhaps even long before we know the Savior very well, we receive intimations of the Spirit that we are important to God, that we are on earth for a divine purpose, and that each one of us is expected to do a great work in the building of the kingdom of God. As the intimations of the Spirit increase, we will become more and more excited about the special and peculiar contributions we can make because of our distinct personalities, talents, and experiences. We will be thrilled and grateful for the variety of remarkable talents we see in our brothers and sisters in the gospel and the way those special talents are effectively used by the Lord in building the kingdom of God, for we will know that in our individuality and uniqueness, we too will have marvelous opportunities to serve in the building of the kingdom and in bringing souls to the Father through Christ.

As we faithfully and determinedly negotiate the straight and narrow path, keeping the basic commandments, I believe the Lord will gradually reveal the special and peculiar things he would have us do. As we become aware of how our lives should unfold according to his divine pleasure we then are able to enjoy the kind of faith that will pull down the very powers of heaven. Incidently, few things in mortal life are more exciting than feeling that our lives are unfolding according to his mind and will.

Sacrifice—Key to the Power of Faith

How can we obtain the power from the Lord that will increase our abilities far above the capabilities of man? The key is sacrifice. I have often felt that when the Lord discovers that we are really serious about going all the way back to the presence of the Father, that we are willing to bear the shame of the world (Jacob 2:8), that we want with all of our hearts to see the Lord while yet in the flesh, that we want to make our calling and election sure, that we desire to have the heavens open to us and know with a perfect knowledge that the path we are following is ordained of God—when he sees that we are totally serious about our commitment to him, he fashions for us a tailor-made cross. The time will come when it will be necessary to take our cross upon ourselves totally and completely with full purpose of heart, and when the full measure of the weight of that cross comes upon us, without exception we will cry out, "Why, oh why is the cross so heavy? It's all I can do to bear up under it, let alone carry it!"

His voice will then come quietly into our hearts: "I made your cross heavy that you might be willing to look to me for the strength to carry it. If you will seek for my help, I will bestow upon you the power you need to carry the cross, and in the process, you will become strong like until myself."

It is the experience of all saints, without exception, who determine to climb all the way to the lofty spiritual peaks of their own Mount Sinais to be quite overwhelmed at the trials, the tribulations, the temptations, and the heavy responsibilities that are theirs. But all of these challenges are part of the great purpose of earth life and if we didn't have them, we wouldn't be able to acquire the faith in Christ we need to be redeemed. For as we take upon ourselves our individual crosses, we will all come to know that the path we must follow is so challenging, the load we must carry so heavy, that the only way we can do it is by obtaining the marvelous sustaining power of the Master in our lives.

A student in one of my classes shared the following dream or vision which illustrated the importance of being willing to take upon ourselves the Savior's cross, that in doing so, we might have the power to come all the way to him.

He said he found himself crossing a desert. It was hot, and he was carrying on his shoulders a very heavy cross. After a while, he became so tired of carrying the cross that he laid it down and sawed off part of it. Having done so, he lifted the cross back on his shoulders and continued his journey. Again, the cross became too heavy, so he laid it down and sawed off another portion. After stopping and sawing off several portions of the cross, he came to a narrow but very deep ravine. As he stood at the edge he looked across, and there, standing on the other side with outstretched arms, was the Savior. As their eyes met, the Savior beckoned and invited him to come to him. However, he indicated to the Savior that he couldn't because the ravine was too wide. The Savior told him to lay the cross he was carrying over the ravine and use it to walk upon. He quickly took the cross, and as he attempted to span the ravine with it, he discovered the cross was too short! At that moment he awakened.

Oh, that you and I would realize that in our allowing heavy responsibilities to be laid upon our shoulders, in our joyfully going through trials and tribulations, in our being willing to try to do the impossible, we will come to know that the Lord is a God of power.

The power to do what the Lord would have us do is in direct proportion to the assurance and confidence we feel coming from him that we are doing what he wants us to do! In fact, Joseph Smith, in *Lectures On Faith* emphasized that such an assurance is an absolute prerequisite to enjoying the power of faith:

Such was, and always will be, the situation of the Saints

of God, that unless they have an actual knowledge that
the course they are pursuing is according to the will of
God they will grow weary in their minds, and faint.

The experiences related in the rest of this chapter have to do
primarily with how the Lord can make bare his mighty arm in
every area of life. I didn't see the hand of the Lord in many of these
experiences until some time after they occurred. In other
instances, the mighty arm of the Lord was unveiled in a most
visible, dramatic miraculous way. But all of the following
experiences and many unmentioned, represent a visibility of the
Lord's kindness, love, and especially his great power that are the
very delight of earth life.

Intimations of Purpose

I remember from the time I was ten years old until I was about
sixteen, one of my favorite things to do in the wintertime was to
leave the house late at night, walk a short distance to the stack
yards, and climb a tall ladder to the top of a haystack. After
brushing aside the snow, I would lie on my back, cover myself
except for my head with hay so I would stay warm, and then just lie
there looking up at the starry heavens. Each time I did that there
distilled into my heart feelings that life was infinitely greater than I
had yet envisioned. The heavens were awesome to me, but it
seemed that I sensed, in spite of the vastness of space and my
seeming insignificance, I was an integral and important part of a
great plan.

After each experience, as I climbed down the ladder, I somehow
was renewed in my feelings of excitement for life. It was hard to
put my finger on what was happening inside, but I knew it was
good.

As I gradually became a little more seasoned in the things of the
Spirit and there seemed to emerge at least a partial blueprint of

what the Lord wanted me to do with my life, I found in the reflections and feelings that had come on those winter nights as I looked up at the heavens a reservoir of meaning and strength that gave me great motivation to try to draw on the Lord's power to help accomplish what otherwise would have seemed totally out of the question.

Acquiring a 20th Century Handcart

As a young fellow, I often felt disappointed that I wasn't born a hundred years or so earlier so I could show my faith and devotion to the Lord by willingly pushing a handcart across the plains. But as my wife and I have had our lives unfold, neither of us have felt any regret for not being sent to the earth as handcart pioneers—our challenges, in fact, have seemed akin to a ten-ton handcart!

Early in our married life, we became aware of three major challenges that seemed destined to tax our faith, our physical stamina, and our finances far beyond their limits. First, there was no question in our minds that we were to have a large family. I had received an explicit prophetic promise in my patriarchal blessing that we would be "blessed with children—not a few." Both my wife and I were totally determined to fulfill that great promise.

Secondly, again with the help of the inspired words of a patriarch and many other unmistakable assurances from the Lord, I knew it was required of me to obtain all the education I could (I say "required" because I was not all that excited about higher education, and I had initially hoped that somehow one year of General Agriculture at Utah State Agricultural College would satisfy the Lord's educational plans for me).

The third challenge emerged as we sensed strongly that the Lord would be pleased if I would pursue my livelihood in Church Education. Now this was a challenge because economically it was very difficult to have a large family and pursue all three degrees on an educator's salary.

With those three challenges, we discovered that we were trying to push a personal handcart that simply was impossible even to move unless we sought for and obtained the power of the Savior himself.

Be Fruitful

Both my wife and I, long before we met each other, came to the conclusion we would honor the counsel of the First Presidency on not postponing or limiting the children who would come into our union. In addition, as mentioned earlier, the Lord revealed to us clearly that he would be pleased if we would have a large family. Nevertheless, it required a tremendous exercise of faith. I was a twenty-five year old sophomore and had married a woman who had no money (like her husband), we had no maternity insurance, and so many well-meaning friends and loved ones continually cautioned us about how hard it would be to have children right away. There was no question in our minds that unless the Lord intervened and blessed us with his strength and power, we simply could not do what we knew was expected of us.

One of the most challenging questions facing any couple and one that surely faced us was how many children to have. There is only one way to know and to obtain the power to have those children and that is through the revelations/blessings of the Lord.

As an example: We had quite a few children and were wondering if we would yet have more when the following experience occurred. As part of family night we decided to draw the floor plans for our dream home. After laying a large sheet of butcher paper on the floor, we commenced sketching out the plan on the basis of input from each of the children. Finally, after adding more and more butcher paper for more and more rooms, I announced that I was ready to count the number or rooms in this palatial dream house. I was about to give the final tabulation when all of a sudden Sweetie said, "Wait a minute, how about when the rest of the children come?" There was a pause as we just looked at each other and there quietly descended upon Diane and I an assurance that the Lord would be pleased if we yet had more children. It was such a simple and yet beautiful distilling of his will to our hearts, and yet from that experience came the strength and determination to have yet another child.

On another occasion the assurance that the Lord was pleased we were willing to have another child came after the baby had arrived. The pregnancy for this particular baby had been unusually hard, and it seemed the whole family had had to sacrifice more than usual.

After the baby was delivered and the day arrived to bring my wife and the new little one home, I felt a special peace and excitement. The timing was beautiful for it was the Lord's day and the children had just arrived home from Church. As I drove up in front of our home, the children, Grandmother, a brother-in-law and other close friends excitedly came running out of the house and the excitement they radiated was really a delight to see. I stood back and watched the scene as the baby was passed from one to another. After we got into the front room and the baby was still being held momentarily by one and then the next, it seemed to me that I became aware that there were others in the room who were witnessing that marvelous welcome. It was as though unseen visitors were rejoicing that she had arrived safely at her new home and especially did they seem to rejoice because the baby was so warmly and gratefully welcomed. The many months when Diane wasn't feeling well, the frustration of finding it hard to keep the house in order, the challenge of doing everything we wanted to do for the children—all of these things seemed at that moment so totally insignificant.

I got everyone's attention and asked them if we could kneel down and express together our appreciation to the Lord for sending us another of his precious offspring. The experience that day in our livingroom was a veil-thinning experience. How totally we knew the Lord had protected, nurtured, and strengthened my wife and the entire family. How totally we knew he was pleased that we had so gratefully welcomed her into our home, and how perfectly we knew there were many unseen loved ones who had come to rejoice in that glorious experience.

All husbands should be most mindful that it is the wife who carries the heavier burden when it comes to having and rearing children, and even though he may do all in his power to help with that burden, unless the wife is strengthened by the Savior, her strength will often not be adequate.

The following experience, written by my wife, shows that God will ease the heavy burden of carrying a child by bestowing the needed power and strength to do his will. She writes:

"When I was expecting our seventh child, I had an experience which has since given me great strength and a divine power to accomplish whatever the Lord would have me do.

We were living in Palo Alto, California, at the time, in a large two story home. It was late one night, my husband was gone and the children had all been tucked in after what I would call 'one of those days.' It seemed that everything had gone wrong! I felt so inadequate and I was sure I was the worst mother in the whole world.

As I started up the stairs to my bedroom to retire, I had thoughts and feelings come in upon me that were so vivid I remember them to this day. We knew the Lord wanted us to have a large family, and I recognized our responsibility to have many children. But I had come to the end of my strength emotionally and physically. All the way up the stairs I kept thinking, "I'm so tired! I'm sick to my stomach! My head aches, my back aches, and my feet ache. It is just too hard! I can't do it any more!" As I prepared for bed, I convinced myself that I must pray in spite of my weariness.

I am so grateful that I had learned before this experience that I could go to my Heavenly Father at any time, for any reason, and he would hear me and answer my prayer. I had also learned to be very specific and openly and honestly pour out my heart to one who loves me with a perfect love, who knows me better than I know myself, and who could give me perfect answers.

I was specific indeed that night; in fact, I complained a bit. My prayer was, in essence, "Heavenly Father, I know we are supposed to have many children, but I can't do it! I'm so tired! I'm sick to my stomach, my head aches, my back aches, and my feet ache. It's just too hard! I can't do it!"

That night as I knelt in prayer, the Lord spoke to me in my heart and mind. I did not hear his voice, but the words came as they so often do when he reveals through his Spirit. We know when it comes from him—it changes our lives and the words are forever written across our hearts. The words that came to me were these: 'My daughter, how can you complain about the small miseries required of you to bring my spirit children into the world and give them birth? If I could just give you a glimpse of the magnificent suffering of your Savior in your behalf that you might have a second birth and come back into my presence.'

The Lord's words chided me a bit, but at the same moment I felt a power come into my whole soul as I received my own personal witness of the great atoning sacrifice of my Savior for me. I felt his godly love for me and my worth in his eyes as I realized he was willing to suffer for me in spite of my weaknesses and often unworthy condition. The power that came was the assurance that I could do anything the Lord required of me, including having more children. If I needed help to get through just one day at a time, that power would be available if I would pay the price to humble myself and plead for his assistance. It has come in that manner. My pregnancies have not become any easier—in fact, the challenge has been increasingly more difficult physically and emotionally with the increasing responsibility of a growing family in numbers and ages, but the help has come. I know it will come to all of us whatever the circumstances, whatever our needs. The power is indeed available as we struggle to discern his mind and will, make every effort to *do* his mind and will, and seek for his power to accomplish what he would have us do."

I can't resist another analogy to put over the point that should the Lord desire you to have many children and should you desire to honor his will that doing so is somewhat akin to skating on thin ice!

I remember coming home from high school late one wintry afternoon and deciding I would like to go ice skating on the Snake River. No one was home and I had an hour before it was time to milk the cows, so I grabbed my skates and hurried through a neighbor's field and down a steep bank to the river. In the middle of the river was a mile-long, narrow island then known as Frenchman's Island. The winter had been quite severe, freezing the ice solid between our side of the river and the island. After quickly pulling on my skates, I skated vigorously over to the island. I noticed that at the west end of the island the ice protruded into the river some distance like a small peninsula. It looked very enticing, and I couldn't resist the urge to go skating down the extended peninsula of ice. It was a thrilling sensation to have water not far away on my right and left and also up ahead! After I had foolishly gone some distance, the ice started cracking—what a horrifying sound and sensation to see cracks darting out in all directions. I quickly realized how foolish I was to be skating so far down the strip of ice, so I tried to reverse my direction. Because by then the ice had become so narrow, I had to make a sharp turn which necessitated slowing down considerably, increasing my weight per cubic inch on the ice and creating in turn even more ominous cracking.

I honestly wondered if I would make it back safely to thicker ice, knowing if I broke through, the chance of survival would be very limited (I could just see myself stumbling through the veil soaking wet!). Finally, though, I did make it back to solid, thick ice—what a relief! I was so overjoyed I wanted to fall down and embrace the ice!

Getting married and having all the children the Lord would like you to have is not unlike skating across a wide river on relatively thin ice. As you and your new spouse go to the edge of the river and pause to put on your skates, well-meaning friends and particularly close loved ones pause in their skating to tell you how risky and hard it is to cross the river successfully (again, to have all the children the Lord would like you to have). Even though you think you're filled with faith and you have taken seriously the counsel of the Prophet and the First Presidency, hearing their well reasoned advice causes you to become quite apprehensive. But breathing deep and feeling a new surge of confidence from the Lord, you start out across the river.

The further you go in trying to fulfill the Lord's will, the more advise is being shouted to you from those who have elected to stay comfortably close to the shore. Many times you hear the ice crack and you wonder if you're going to break through and be swallowed up in the river. But the more the ice cracks the more you hold on to each other and the more your prayers ascend to God. Many times at what seems to be the last moment, when it appears that surely you will break through the ice and drown, the Lord reaches down, makes bare his mighty arm, and lifts you on to safer ice. You don't get halfway across the river but what you both marvel at the power and love of your Redeemer.

There is no decision made by a husband and wife that is a deeper pledge of their love for each other and their confidence in the power of a divine Redeemer than the decision to have all the children the Lord would be pleased to send to their union. Many beautiful things have happened in our lives, things that have manifested to us how great God is, but none have shown us the Lord's mercy, his goodness, his power, and his love as has his enabling us to have and take care of the children he has been pleased to send us.

Struggling By Degrees

There were a lot of reasons why I thoroughly enjoyed my high school days—football, skiing, tumbling and track, to name a few, as well as a vigorous social life and heavy involvement in student government. Those reasons, incidentally, were the very same reasons why I wasn't very serious about academics! And as if I didn't have enough distractions, there were the twenty cows that needed to be milked every morning and night, and the farm work to be done in the spring and fall while school was yet in session. I felt fortunate to have survived academically as well as I did, but part of the price I paid for all my extracurricular activities was that I didn't think college was all that important and that perhaps one year would be more than enough.

Although I didn't recognize it until I came home, my mission brought into focus an ignored request in my patriarchal blessing to "obtain all the education you can." Again, an awareness of what the Lord wanted me to do began to crystallize in my heart and with it came the assurance that in spite of poor study habits and not having the foggiest notion what I should study, it was imperative I return to school and obtain a college degree.

My classes at the "Y" immediately set both my mind and my spirit on fire, and I really became excited about the desire to excel. I picked a major, but wasn't sure what I would actually do for a livelihood. However, I did have the assurance that I was at least going the right direction. All the while, I was praying a lot and seeking with all of my heart for inspiration as to specifically what I needed to do to prepare for a profession.

Although I didn't realize the far reaching implication of what was happening, I did notice that I was infinitely more interested in and fascinated by what I was learning in my religion classes than all the other classes I was taking. Also, I had been invited to be a Sunday School teacher in what was then "campus branch" and that one experience gave me a taste for teaching and a desire to teach that became the mainspring determining my life's work.

Much to our disappointment, after only a brief stay at the "Y" it became necessary to return to the farm to help my father whose health was failing him. How hard it was to leave! I so desperately wanted to move vigorously ahead on my degree and I felt I needed to take some classes to help me decide what I should do—but that wasn't the game plan. The stage was set effectively to give us the very answers we were seeking; indeed, we were to learn that "the Lord moves in mysterious ways his wonders to perform." We had only been home for months when I was invited to teach full-time seminary! I taught just a few weeks when I knew with all of my heart that I wanted to teach in the Church Educational System on a permanent basis. Again, the assurance that came to me that my life was unfolding as the Lord would have it unfold brought a sense of purpose and a degree of motivation that I don't think could have come in any other way.

The joy and satisfaction of teaching seminary became the propelling influence to motivate me to persist in getting my education. I knew the Lord wanted me to get my education, but not having developed the study skills as fully as I should have, and with children coming at quite frequent intervals, and there never being enough money to pay all the bills, I needed desperately the assurance from the Lord that I must persist in obtaining my schooling in spite of the tremendous challenges.

And frequent assurances that we were doing what the Lord wanted us to do did come. One such experience that had a real impact on me occurred during a summer session of school. We were living in Wyview Village, which was university housing for married couples. The individual houses had at one time been used as housing for Mountain Home Air Force Base in Idaho. In my earlier years on the farm, I had watched those houses being hauled along US 30, never dreaming that some day I would live in one. Whoever designed the houses probably didn't realize that in the summer they were nothing more than family size saunas! Oh they were hot! In addition, we were living on a shoe string, Diane was expecting, and all in all the circumstances were somewhat challenging.

I was in the Joseph Smith Auditorium with several hundred seminary and institute men listening to a talk by Elder A. Theodore Tuttle. His talk was on commitment, and while he was speaking, there came a marvelous assurance that my wife and I were doing exactly what the Lord wanted us to do. It was really a powerful assurance. When Elder Tuttle finished, I hurried over to the little house, ran into the kitchen and threw my arms around my wife. The Spirit I had felt while in the auditorium seemed to return as I shared with Diane my feelings. She knew as I did that what I was saying was true, and we were both encouraged and strengthened.

The hardest challenge in terms of getting a degree came when we decided to launch into a doctoral program at the "Y". At the time we made the decision, we were living in Palo Alto, California, where I was directing the Institute of Religion adjacent to Stanford University. The experience there was especially enjoyable. We loved the beauty of the entire bay area, and the intellectual stimulation we found on campus was a delight. However, economically, it was impossible! Even though we were as careful as we could be, we were sinking further and further into debt.

I remember that when the idea of applying for sabbatical leave first came into my mind, my greatest concern was financial. I recall indicating to the Lord that we hadn't been able to live on a full salary, and I wasn't sure how we would live on the reduced sabbatical salary. As I inquired, I didn't get much comfort, just the strong confirmation I should do it! I was really concerned because our debts had increased as had the number of our children (we now had seven) and all of us were so addicted to food!

But I made the application, the sabbatical was granted, we moved to Provo and I commenced work on the doctorate. As the year progressed, I had a strong assurance that we were right where we should be, and I was doing exactly what I should be doing. However, our economic situation continued to worsen so much that I felt there would be no way we could continue under those circumstances another year. However, as I prayed mightily to the Lord, I felt an overriding peace that somehow things would work out.

When summer arrived, I readily accepted my first invitation to do Education Weeks in Arizona and Texas, knowing it would supplement the income a little. The expenses for the trip—money for motels, food and travel—were sent ten days in advance, and I simply couldn't resist the temptation to use at least part of it to meet current needs.

The day before I was to leave I was feeling extremely anxious about how tight our circumstances were, when I went to check the mail. There was a letter from a choice couple in another state. I opened it and it read in part: "We appreciate deeply what you are doing—we admire your determination to return to school for the doctorate. We feel it's wonderful you are willing to have a large family, and we are grateful you have stayed in Church Education. Some time ago, we told the Lord that if he would bless us in a particular investment, we would share with you a portion of the returns on that investment. The Lord has blessed us, and enclosed is a check for the first payment of your portion we promised the Lord we would share with you. Please do not feel obligated to thank us for it. It was the Lord who made it possible."

I pulled the enclosed check out of the envelope and could hardly believe my eyes as I looked at the amount of that blessing. I ran excitedly into the house and found Sweetie talking on the phone to a good friend. As I somewhat enthusiastically did back hand-springs and cartwheels, it occurred to her that perhaps I had something important to say to her. She hung up the phone, and I put my arms around her, showed her the check and read her the letter.

As we held on to each other tightly and "wept a few tears", there came into our hearts a perfect knowledge that we were doing exactly what the Lord wanted us to do, and that he had heard our prayers and opened the way so we could accomplish that which we knew we should do. It was still a tremendous struggle to get the doctorate, but in the meantime, we were having all the children the Lord wanted us to have, Sweetie did not have to work outside the home and all in all, we knew that the Lord had heard our prayers and blessed us with power in ways we never dreamed possible.

Be It Ever So Humble

One of the greatest challenges facing most couples is buying a home. In no area of our lives was the marvelous power of the Lord made more evident than in our obtaining our home. Perhaps to appreciate how marvelous that manifestation of power was, it would help to be aware of one of the first places we lived as a young married couple.

When my wife and I left school to return to the farm to help Dad, we moved into a little three-room house on the farm. I use the word "house" loosely because the house was so loose. It had been built in 1909 without a foundation. When we moved in, it got its first painting. There was running water (a creek ran along in front of the house), and the bathroom consisted of four walls and a path. It didn't matter if the windows were open or closed, the velocity of the Idaho wind through the house was about the same, making it next to impossible to keep the house warm—we had to hang blankets over the door into the tiny front room and bedroom just to keep adequate heat in the kitchen. We heated the water, both to do the dishes and to bathe, with an electrical heating unit. We bathed in an oblong galvanized tin tub. For our Saturday night bath, we would put some water in the tub on Thursday, put the heating unit in the water, and by Saturday night the water would be at least body temperature. As we struggled and gradually were able to get a hot water heater and replace the hot plate with an electrical range and build on a little bathroom, we both acquired a sense of appreciation for the niceties of life that up to then we had always taken for granted.

After teaching for a year and a half at the "Y", I was invited to join the faculty. With that invitation came the realization that we could finally settle down and buy our own home after wandering to and fro for fifteen years. It had been a difficult experience to find rental homes in the valley of adequate size for a large family.

Being extremely busy with my graduate program, a heavy teaching load and a sizable church calling, I found a ready excuse not to spend much time searching the want ads and tromping the pavement in search of permanent living quarters. In fact, when I did turn myself to the task, it was half-hearted, perhaps for two reasons: one was that I felt strongly that when the "right time" came, the necessary doors would open to enable us to obtain a home; and second, we had managed to maintain quite consistently a zero balance in our savings account.

To illustrate the idea of the "right time" concept, I remember how excited we were when a friend offered to sell us a building lot in the north end of the valley at a very fair price. Without specifically clearing the decision with the Lord (isn't it obvious that everyone needs to buy a home?) we successfully obtained a down payment from the credit union and drove to the alumni camp at Aspen Grove to meet our friend and close the transaction.

As my wife and I drove alone to make the appointment, I felt heavy and negative about what we were doing. It was difficult to sort out my feelings. I knew we desperately needed a home, that the deal we were to make was fair, and that Diane had evidenced great joy at the prospect of having our own home. Yet I felt that indeed I shouldn't close the deal.

We didn't talk much during the 30 minute drive up the canyon. Much to our surprise, the good brother who was to meet us didn't show up. We waited till quite late, then drove back down the canyon. The heavy negative feelings persisted. I wanted to stop the car, look my wife right in the eyes and say, "I don't know why, but we are not supposed to buy that lot and build a home there!" but I didn't have the nerve—I thought surely she would be devastated with disappointment.

I spent a restless night, and when I awakened in the morning, it was abundantly clear in my mind that we should forget building a home right then. I awakened my wife, put my arms around her, and told her what I felt we should do. When I did, she squealed with delight and said, "That's exactly how I feel, and I felt that way when we went up the canyon, but I just couldn't bring myself to tell you, because I was afraid you'd be so disappointed!"

Months later, as I finished giving a final exam, I was chatting with one of my students from California. Among other things, I told her how excited we were that we would be settling down in Provo. She responded, "Why don't you buy Dad's home here in Provo? It's up for sale." I casually asked, "Where is it?" She told me it was on the east bench above the temple.

I then attempted to conclude that part of the conversation without divulging any economic limitations on our part by saying simply, "We really wouldn't be interested in looking at homes in that particular area"—a fairly veiled way of telling her there was no way we could afford a home in that section of the city. But she was persistent: she later brought me a penciled drawing of the floor plan of the house, and she kept insisting that we at least come and look at the house.

Several weeks later, somewhat on a lark and yet feeling impressed to do it, I asked my wife if she would like to ride up and at least look at "that" house. She said she would, and anyway, we did have friends in Idaho who had told us to keep our eyes open for a house they might buy.

I called the realtor and made an appointment for that morning. As we drove up, we noticed that the realtor had parked her Cadillac in front of the house. Considering the appearance of our car, I wondered if perhaps it wouldn't be appropriate to park some distance down the street.

We were met at the door by a very gracious woman who indicated she was the realtor. As we walked into the hallway, I really got excited—I honestly had the feeling something very important was happening. In fact, I felt as though we were coming home and that the house had been made just for us!

About half-way through the tour, while we were in the family room downstairs, the daughter of the owners came bouncing in with several friends who were roommates in the house. These roommates I had also had in classes, and they all seemed pleasantly surprised and pleased to see us. The realtor then made the connection between who I was and previous information as to how the owners felt about me, which, much to my relief, was most positive! In making that connection, the realtor seemed to increase in her zeal to convince me I should buy the home.

While I felt so much at home in the house and had strong intimations that somehow great things were about to happen, those feelings were offset by knowing we had no savings for a down payment and my salary was not adequate to continue payments each month. In fact, I was convinced that had the realtor known our economic situation, she probably wouldn't have shown us the house.

Still, the excitement in my heart increased as I looked for the right moment, then inquired about the price. As she told us, much of the excitment left. We couldn't afford that much, and I said so. She nevertheless encouraged me to make an offer. I hesitated, but the realtor persisted, so finally I did make an offer. The look on her face seemed to suggest I should perhaps make another offer. But then, with a gleam in her eye, she said boldly, "I've done a lot of crazy things—I will call the owner and tell him what you've offered." Amazed at her bravado, I indicated that would be fine.

Sweetie and I then got in the car and started to drive down into the valley. She looked at me just a little teary eyed and said quietly, "What do you think?" I replied that as ridiculous as it seemed, I honestly felt the offer would be accepted and the home would be ours.

The next day, the realtor called, and with a great deal of excitement, informed us the owner had accepted our offer! The following Monday night, we took the children over to see the house. While we were there, the daughter called her parents and by phone we became acquainted with the owners for the first time. They seemed so excited that we were going to buy their home. During the conversation, the owners said they would like us to have the couch in the front room as a house warming gift. We were so pleased and grateful—in fact, my wife and I had concluded that were we to haul our old couch into such a nice home, we would surely be struck with lightning! (We had a family ritual we went through whenever people would come to see us: at a given signal, the children would run through the bedrooms gathering blankets and pillows and cover the couch totally so that the arriving guests who sat on the couch would not be mortally wounded.

After graciously giving us the couch, the owners indicated they didn't want to haul the furniture back to California and would we be interested in buying all or part of it? (Incidentally, every room of the five-bedroom house was totally furnished and included two TV sets, a lovely stereo, and a ping pong table.) We excitedly told him we would be most interested.

At this point, there was also the challenge of obtaining what to us was an immense down payment. Again, the Lord intervened and the down payment was miraculously provided.

In the early summer, the owners came to Provo to close the deal. They generously took us to dinner, and as the evening ended, the owner asked if we had decided what furniture we wanted to buy and how much we would be willing to pay for it. I told him we wanted essentially all of it, but hadn't decided on what we could pay. He asked if we would make an offer by the following morning.

We struggled that evening with that decision—we didn't want to be unfair, and yet we still didn't have any money. The following morning as we met the owners in the home, they handed us a large card that said "God bless our mortgaged furniture." As they handed us the card, they laughed. It was hard for us to laugh with them! The four of us slipped into the master bedroom when I screwed up my courage and said,"We will be happy to pay you $1,000 for the furniture if we can have two years to pay it off." They started laughing again, which, to say the least, was a bit perplexing. Then the owner said, "You'll do no such thing—$350 is plenty for the furniture.

Even now, many years later, both my wife and I are still quite overwhelmed at the way the Lord provided a home and furniture for us. Many times when I have hurried home during the noon hour for lunch, as I entered the house there would come such a wave of appreciation over me for having a home that I would grab Diane by the hand, we would kneel, and together we would express deeply our appreciation for our home and for all the blessings the Lord has given us.

Be it the getting of our home, obtaining the degrees, or having and raising the children the Lord has sent us, in all things the Savior's power has been made manifest in our lives in a marvelous way.

In the 133rd section of the Doctrine and Covenants there is a great concept that expresses beautifully the feelings of gratitude I feel for the goodness of the Lord. As the Savior descends in glory at his second coming, he speaks of the tremendous importance of his atonement—that he did tread the winepress alone and sprinkled the blood of the unrepentant upon his garments (verses 50-51). But then he speaks to those who are redeemed by him—those who have their garments washed white in the blood of the Lamb and he says: "And they the redeemed shall mention the loving kindness of their Lord, and all that he has bestowed upon them according to his goodness, and according to his loving kindness, forever and ever." (verse 52.) The one central thought that will be in our minds and hearts when the triumphant Christ returns to the earth in great glory will be our gratitude for his many kindnesses to us.

The impact of that idea came very powerfully to my wife and me one sabbath evening in the summertime. Our meetings were over and the children seemed to be occupied in worthwhile activities, so I took Diane by the hand and invited her to walk up the mouth of Rock Canyon with me. We came to a huge rectangular shaped boulder and decided to climb up on it and together watch the sun go down.

As we sat there close together, quite thrilled with the beauty of our surroundings, our conversation turned to the Lord. We both spontaneously talked about experience after experience where he had bestowed upon us in such marvelous ways blessing after blessing. I don't know that I had ever felt more deeply the reality of his blessings in our lives. We were both deeply moved and so anxious to do all in our power to honor him.

The Lord is God! He is a God of great love and mighty miracles. He does want to reveal to us his mind and will. He does want to give each one of us a divine sense of destiny and bestow upon all of us the blessings we need to realize that marvelous destiny.

> And a voice came out of the throne, saying, Praise our God, all ye his servants, and ye that fear him, both small and great. And I heard as it were the voice of a great multitude, and as the voice of many waters, and as the voice of mighty thunderings, saying, Alleluia! (Revelations 19:5-6.)

Chapter 8

To Know The Lord Is To Recognize And Accept His Living Prophets

A few days prior to the Savior's atoning sacrifice there occurred an extremely touching scene in his life. As he stood in the holy city of Jerusalem, a city he loved so much, he paused and "then Jesus began to weep over Jerusalem, saying, O Jerusalem! Jerusalem! Ye who will kill the prophets, and will stone them who are sent unto you; how often would I have gathered your children together, even as a hen gathers her chickens under her wings, and ye would not." (I.V. Matthew 23:36-37.)

The Savior, in this moving declaration, confirms one of the most important doctrines of his gospel, and that is that holy prophets, called and ordained of him, have the sacred role of bringing individuals to him. From Adam on, it has always been holy prophets of God who have extended the Lord's invitation for mankind to come to him. If living prophets do not extend that invitation, the invitation is made in vain.

Prophets at the beginning of each dispensation are called, prepared, and enabled to perform their sacred responsibilities in this way: The prophet is given the marvelous opportunity of being introduced to the Savior by seeing and conversing with him face to face. This introduction is invariably made by God the Father himself. (James E. Talmage, *Jesus the Christ*, p. 39) After the prophet receives a perfect knowledge that Jesus is the Christ, the step that usually follows is the visitation of angelic beings who reveal more fully the mind and will of the Savior to him. In the course of these angelic manifestations not only is instruction given but the holy priesthood is bestowed, the necessary ordinances are performed, and the prophet receives all the priesthood keys and powers he needs to enable him to invite the residue of God's children to come to Christ (Moroni 7:31-31). The ordained and endowed prophet then moves among as many people as he can, testifying in the power and spirit of the Holy Ghost of what he has seen, heard and received. As he does so, those who hear and who are lovers of truth will allow the Holy Ghost to have place in their hearts, and they will accept the words of the prophet and embrace the heaven-sent message. In time, through their faithfulness, they, like the prophets, may come to a perfect knowledge of Christ by seeing and conversing with him.

When Joseph's sacred grove experience was over, he could return to his home, lean up next to the fireplace, and with fixed determination and a marvelous power, plant in his mother's heart the seeds for a redemptive faith as he declared, "I have learned for myself that Presbyterianism is not true!" His testimony, charged by the power of the Holy Ghost, rang in her ears. "I have learned for myself!" He did not say, "I believe," or "I think," but with emphasis, "I have learned for myself!" (Carter E. Grant, *The Kingdom of God Restored*, Salt Lake City: Deseret Book, 1965, p. 28.) With that witness imbued in her heart, the prophet's mother, like countless others, grew in the testimony, knowledge, and power of Christ.

Simply put, even though in our day the Christian world has access to the Bible and has thousands of well-read and well-meaning ministers and priests who have taught the scriptures to the best of their ability, they could not and never will be able to distill in the hearts of their followers a redeeming faith in Christ because they have not seen Christ, have not been commissioned of him, and cannot speak with authority in declaring his mind and will.

The Doctrine and Covenants indicate that Moses is a prototype of the ancient prophets and that Joseph Smith as well as each succeeding prophet is to us as Moses was to the children of Israel. Let's consider that relationship in a little more detail.

The Lord made a remarkable promise to Moses when he said Moses would "be made stronger than many waters; for they shall obey thy command as if thou wert God." (Moses 1:25; emphasis added.) On another occasion, the Lord told Moses that as he fulfilled his calling and used Aaron as his mouthpiece, he, Moses, would be as God to Aaron (Exodus 4:16). What a remarkable position for Moses to hold—to be as God to the children of Israel.

In our day, the Lord has told us that Joseph is to us as Moses was to the children of Israel (D&C 28:2), and we know we have received the word of the Lord through him (D&C 5:10). The Lord tells us further that the President of the office of the High Priesthood (the prophet, seer, and revelator to the Church) is to "preside over the whole Church, and to be like unto Moses."

Brigham said of Joseph Smith:

> No man or woman in this dispensation will ever enter into the celestial kingdom of God without the consent of Joseph Smith. From the day that the Priesthood was taken from the earth to the winding-up scene of all things, every man and woman must have the certificate of Joseph Smith, Junior, as a passport to their entrance into the mansion where God and Christ are—I with you and you with me. I cannot go there without his consent. He holds the keys of that kingdom for the last dis-

pensation (Brigham Young, *JD* 7:289)

In another address, President Young shared deeply additional feelings about the Prophet Joseph which I believe reflect a confidence and faith in God's prophets that need to be emulated by all the Saints:

> And were I to be asked whether I have any experience in this matter, I can tell the people that once in my life I felt a want of confidence in brother Joseph Smith, soon after I became acquainted with him. It was not concerning religious matters—it was not about his revelations—but it was in relation to his financiering—to his managing the temporal affairs which he undertook. A feeling came over me that Joseph was not right in his financial management, though I presume the feeling did not last sixty seconds, and perhaps not thirty. But that feeling came on me once and once only, from the time I first knew him to the day of his death. It gave me sorrow of heart, and I clearly saw and understood, by the spirit of revelation manifested to me, that if I was to harbor a thought in my heart that Joseph could be wrong in anything, I would begin to lose confidence in him, and that feeling would grow from step to step, and from one degree to another, until at last I would have the same lack of confidence in his being the mouthpiece for the Almighty. . . . Though I admitted in my feelings and knew all the time that Joseph was a human being and subject to err, still it was none of my business to look after his faults.
>
> I repented of my unbelief, and that too, very suddenly; I repented about as quickly as I committed the error. It was not for me to question whether Joseph was dictated by the Lord at all times and under all circumstances or not. I never had the feeling for one moment, to believe that any man or set of men or beings upon the face of the

whole earth had anything to do with him, for he was superior to them all, and held the keys of salvation over them. Had I not thoroughly understood this and believed it, I much doubt whether I should ever have embraced what is called "Mormonism." He was called of God; God dictated him, and if He had a mind to leave him to himself and let him commit an error, that was no business of mine. And it was not for me to question it, if the Lord was disposed to let Joseph lead the people astray, for He had called him and instructed him to gather Israel and restore the Priesthood and kingdom to them.

It was not my prerogative to call him in question with regard to any act of his life. He was God's servant and not mine. He did not belong to the people but to the Lord, and was doing the work of the Lord, and if He should suffer him to lead the people astray, it would be because they ought to be led astray. If He should suffer them to be chastised, and some of them destroyed, it would be because they deserved it, or to accomplish some righteous purpose. That was my faith, and it is my faith still. (Brigham Young, *JD* 4:297-298.)

There should be no question how the Lord views the prophets of our dispensation, and what he expects of us in accepting them as his literal mouthpiece. Even as Christ is the manifestation of the mind and will of God, so are his chosen holy prophets the manifestation of his mind and will.

Watersheds

The term "watershed" is used in geography to describe a whole region from which a river receives its supply of water. When it rains on the Continental Divide or Rocky Mountains, that rain which falls on the western slopes will end up in an entirely different river system than that which falls on the eastern slopes. The same term is also used in philosophy to describe a dividing point of juncture in an area of philosophical thought.

There are also great issues in the Church that can be seen as religious watersheds. How we view the prophet is perhaps one of the greatest. Both in and out of the Church, it is a comparatively easy thing to profess faith in Christ and a willingness to do what he would have us do as long as we determine what we think he wants us to do. But to accept the Savior on his terms as revealed clearly through his prophets is an entirely different matter, and a most difficult one. It can indeed be said to be a dividing line between true believers and non-believers.

Somehow, most people of the Christian world love dead prophets much more than they do living prophets. There are so many on earth today who "do not desire that the Lord their God . . . should rule and reign over them." (Helaman 12:6) I have often wondered why people are so resistive to the concept of living prophets and have concluded that it is because first of all, living prophets have a marvelous way of removing the mystery which surrounds God, Christ, and the gospel, which to many people is unbelievably disquieting for it leaves them no excuse as to what is expected of them. Another reason seems to be that living prophets invariably speak clearly and forcibly on current contemporary issues, be they political, social, economical, or spiritual, and what they have to say is so often the opposite of what those who love the world are saying. In addition, it is much, much easier to misquote and/or misconstrue what dead prophets have said—and get away with it—than it is to misquote or misconstrue what living prophets are saying.

Using the idea of watersheds there are several areas that seem to cause a struggle for some Saints. Three of the most common are:

Does the prophet have the right to give directions to the Saints on any subject, be it social, economical, political, or religious?

Is it within the realm of possibility for the Lord through his prophet to give a command that contradicts an earlier command?

Is it possible, if we are totally obedient to the revelations of the current prophet to become completely united and be as one in every phase of political, economic, social, and religious life?

The answers we give to these questions are most important in determining if we really believe in and sustain the Lord's prophets.

No Dividing Line Between the Spiritual and the Temporal

Few things cause some Saints to be more upset than the prophet giving direction in the temporal aspects of life, especially as that direction relates to the social issues of our day. Be it concerning prohibition, right to work, counsel as to the kind of people we should vote for, the welfare state or E.R.A., invariably there is an upsurge of criticism. Such has probably always been the case. Brigham Young observed:

> Some of the leading men in Kirtland were much opposed to Joseph the Prophet, meddling with temporal affairs, they did not believe that he was capable, of dictating to the people upon temporal matters, thinking that his duty embraced spiritual things alone, and that the people should be left to attend to their temporal affairs, without any interference whatever from Prophets or Apostles. Men in authority there, would contend with Joseph on this point, not openly, but in their little Councils. After a while the matter culminated into a public question; it became so public that it was in the mouth of almost every one. In a public meeting of the Saints, I said "Ye Elders of Israel, Father Smith is present, the Prophet is present, and here are his counselors, here are also High Priests and Elders of Israel, now, will some of you draw the line

of demarcation, between the spiritual and the temporal in the Kingdom of God, so that I may understand it?" Not one of them could do it. When I saw a man stand in the path before the Prophet to dictate to him, I felt like hurling him out the way and branding him as a fool. . . .

I defy any man on earth to point out the path a Prophet of God should walk in, or point out his duty, and just how far he must go, indictating temporal or spiritual things. Temporal and spiritual things are inseperably connected, and ever will be. (Brigham Young, *JD* 10:363-4.)

President J. Reuben Clark expressed similar sentiments:

I call your attention to the fact that there is no limitation to the matters to be covered by the scriptures on which the Lord speaks. . . . Having in mind that this Church is a practical Church and deals with temporal as well as spiritual affairs, I submit that whatever comes from the voices of those who hold that authority is scripture, no matter what they speak, that conclusion to me is inevitable. Anything, and everything that affects the well-being of us Latter-day Saints or that has to do with our religion may become a part of that scripture, and when the servants of God speak to us about such things, speaking under the inspiration of the Lord, then their words become scripture. (President J. Reuben Clark as quoted by President Harold B. Lee in "The Place of the Church," an address given to Seminary and Institute faculty at BYU, June 24, 1960.)

One would think that almost everyone who has reflected seriously on the subject would draw the conclusion that man in and of himself is incapable of solving the perilous problems confronting us. We have witnessed millions of people lose their freedoms to totalitarian forms of government. We are aware that the brightest economists in the world can't solve even the most basic economic problems of the country. I think we all marvel that the supreme legal powers in the land have somehow succeeded in giving more concern, protection, and rights to the criminal than the person who is victimized. And we are astounded that the government seemingly can see no relationship between the welfare state and the imminent bankruptcy of our nation. Our dilemma reminds me of the following words of Joseph Smith:

> "Other attempts to promote universal peace and happiness in the human family have proved abortive; every effort has failed; every plan and design has fallen to the ground; it needs the wisdom of God, the intelligence of God, and the power of God to accomplish this." (DHC 5:64.)

There is, then, a resolution to the problems facing us, but it is an unpopular solution and one many think is too slow and ponderous—and that resolution is the recognition that only as we heed the mind and will of the Savior as revealed to his living prophets will we be redeemed temporally as well as spiritually.

"Whatever Jehovah Commands is Right"

The second question posed is: "Is it within the realm of possibility for the Lord through his prophet to give a command that contradicts an earlier command?" We speak of Abrahamic tests in the Church, of being asked, as was Abraham, to do things that are inconsistent with previous commandments—to do things that seem illogical and unreasonable. Often it is hard to understand why the Lord would give such commandments. But can a person's faith truly be tested without such challenging commands? To walk by faith is to walk not by sight, but by revelation. To be obedient to God in Abrahamic tests is to be obedient not because we can understand what he wants us to do, not because it makes sense, but because we know God has asked us to do it!

Perhaps the greatest and possibly the hardest lesson for Joseph Smith to learn was that God can command and revoke at his pleasure (D&C 56:4), as was the case when he commanded that Jackson County should be built up, and then revoked that command. On one occasion, Joseph summed up that principle by saying, "Whatever God requires is right, no matter what it is, although we may not see the reason thereof till long after the events transpire." (*DHC* 5:135.) Joseph further stated, "A man would command his son to dig potatoes and saddle his horse, but before he had done either he would tell him to do something else. This is all considered right; but as soon as the Lord gives a commandment and revokes that decree and commands something else, then the Prophet is considered fallen." (*DHC* 4:478).

I've watched with interest many an Arab potter in Israel fashion vessels according to his desire. The potter knows the vessel he wants to create, he knows how to do it, and he knows the kind of clay he needs to accomplish his task. On occasion, the clay he uses will not yield to the gentle pressure of his fingers, and without a pause, he removes it from the wheel and casts it into a nearby basket. In time, the potter returns to the basket of clay, and with the addition of different components and much working with the clay, he makes it so it is totally responsive to his every wish so that he can fashion it into the vessel he desires.

We must be like clay in the potter's hand. The Savior is the potter. He wants to make us a holy vessel. He knows how to do it—he knows how willing we must be to yield our hearts to his will as manifested through his prophets. He also knows if we aren't willing to give our free agency to him totally and do anything and everything he wants us to do, we cannot be fashioned as he wants us to be.

When a person has a revealed testimony that this work is the work of God, then whatever is required of him—be it to accept the ordination of Seventies to High Priests, the conferral of the priesthood on all worthy males, or the altering of the temple garment—it is of no moment or consequence. The only important things are that we know that God is at the helm of his Church, that his mind and will are moment by moment being made known through the Prophet and the First Presidency, and that we be obedient to whatever he commands!

"If Ye Are Not One You Are Not Mine"

The third question that seems to cause some Saints to stumble is "Is it possible, if we are totally obedient to the revelations of the current prophet, to become completely united and be as one on every phase of political, economic, social, and religious life?

The intercessory prayer uttered by the Savior just hours before his crucifixion had as its great theme the oneness of the Father and the Son and the hope that those who believe in him would be one with them. The Savior further stated that he dwelt in the Father and the Father in him, and he hoped he might dwell in us; if he did, we would be one with him and the Father. (John 17:21, 23.)

In a revelation given in our day, the Savior further stated, "If ye are not one ye are not mine." (D&C 38:27.) I believe with all of my heart that if the Savior dwells in us and we in him, we will be one politically, socially, economically, and spiritually. I believe that we will be one with the prophet in all the above areas as much as the counselors in the First Presidency, the Twelve, and all the General Authorities are one with the Prophet in every aspect of building the kingdom. I know there have been times when the General Authorities have not seen eye to eye on political and other social issues, but these instances are the exception and do not in any way negate the basic premise.

There are those who feel that if the Brethren were to tell us everything we should do, it would rob us of our free agency. What foolishness! When the Father constantly informed the Son of his will, did it rob Christ of his free agency? No! Our free agency would not be trammeled upon unless the Church forced us to accept the course of action it outlines.

The Lord wants to free us totally from sin and ignorance, from spiritual and temporal bondage. Much of the thrust of the gospel of Jesus Christ is to change men's hearts and minds so totally that as a group of faithful saints we are one with God and Christ under the direction of the prophets. Only in that oneness, will we eradicate all evil and enjoy a utopian society.

Pride, Sin: Roots of Criticism

We had a creek on our farm which was created by bubbling springs which originated on our land. Often on hot days we would pause from hoeing beets or hauling hay to run down to the creek, lie down on our stomachs, and drink from a spring. Inasmuch as the creek went through a pasture where there were horses and cows, we went without fail directly to one of the springs instead of the creek itself, for we knew the water would be pure.

So also it is in the Church. We have a fountain of living water to drink from, and how wise we are to drink from the fountain itself instead of downstream where pollutions inevitably will occur.

One of the greatest pollutions that keep us from enjoying pure water from the stream of living water is the pollution of criticizing the Lord's anointed. One of the main sources of this criticism is pride that comes from intellectual attainments.

Let me share an insight that came to me years ago while acting as an Institute Director. The most startling difference between teaching on the high school level and the college level was a quick awareness that on the university level some of the Saints were much more open in their criticism of the prophets. It was quite an eye opener for me to become aware that some of the Brethren were continually criticized and even openly rejected by Saints associated with the local academic community who seemed extremely proud of their academic achievement.

The critics of whom I speak were basically good people and all of them were active in the Church. Initially I assumed that the difference in how they felt about the Brethren and how others felt about the Brethren was mostly a matter of semantics and that if we kept a dialogue open long enough, we would come to realize that our faith and confidence in the prophets was really the same. But such was not the case. The differences were real, things were viewed from two whole different perspectives.

Nephi, seeing and describing the religious condition of our times, spoke strongly against the corruptions and abominations which he saw, including a tendency of some saints to teach the precepts of men instead of the Gospel, when he said, "They have all gone astray save it be a few, who are the humble followers of Christ; nevertheless, they are led, that in many instances *they do err because they are taught the precepts of men.*" (2 Nephi 28:14; emphasis added.)

All of this dispensation's prophets have warned of this problem that confronts the Church. The following two quotes from President Lee are representative of hundreds of quotes that are available:

> Beware of the sophistry of the Gentiles. We have gone through, and are going through a period that we might call sophistication. I do not know what that word (sophistry) means either, but it generally means that there are so many confounded smart people that they are unwilling to listen to the humble prophets of the Lord, and we have suffered from that, and it is a rather severe test through which we are passing. (Harold B. Lee, BYU Devotional Address, February 1962.)

> One of the greatest threats to the work of the Lord today comes from false educational ideas. There is a growing tendency of teachers within and without the Church to make academic interpretations of gospel teachings—to read, as a prophet-leader has said, by the "lamp of their own conceit." Unfortunately, much in the sciences, the arts, politics, and the entertainment field,

as has been well said by an eminent scholar, is "all dominated by this humanistic approach which ignores God and his word as revealed through the prophets." (*CR* October 1968, p. 59.)

Higher education can be, and most of the time is, such a blessing to the Saints. And yet when some Saints take great pride in having a PhD understanding in their field of learning but have only an elementary understanding of the gospel, it is invariably a double challenge for them to view life and their profession through the revelations of the prophets, instead of viewing the revelations of the prophets through the lens of their academic training.

While there are undoubtedly many roots of criticism besides intellectual pride, few things fuel a tendency toward deep and devastating criticism as does sin. Korihor, one of the anti-Christs in the Book of Mormon, was surely steeped in immorality, for he was successful in "leading many women, and also men, to commit whoredoms." (Alma 30:18.) He also was a sign seeker, which, according to the Savior, is one of the characteristics of a wicked and adulterous generation (Matthew 16:4).

President Lee observed:

> There are some who look upon the leaders of this Church and God's anointed as men who are possessed of selfish motives. By them the words of our leaders are always twisted to try to bring a snare to the work of the Lord. Mark well those who speak evil of the Lord's annointed, for they speak from impure hearts. Only the "pure in heart" see the "God" or the divine in man and accept our leaders and accept them as prophets of the living God. (Harold B. Lee, CR October 1947, p. 67.)

One experience might illustrate what I'm attempting to say. A particularly bright young man in an Institute class I taught, incessantly gave me a bad time about almost everything I said. I had put forth some effort to persuade him to take the class. However, because of his attitude and its negative impact on class, I began wondering if I shouldn't persuade him to drop the class!

One beautiful spring day as the students were dismissed, I asked the contentious one if he would be pleased to stay for a while so we could talk alone. We sat out by a fountain, and as I tried to persuade him to be more accepting of the doctine of the Church, he continued to argue with sophistication against everything I said. It was frustrating—I felt such a love for the young man, yet I felt I could easily wring his neck! His arguments were well thought out and reflected powerfully the wisdom of men.

All of a sudden it was made known to me that the young man was immoral. It came so suddenly and with such force that I simply blurted out, "Young man, are you immoral?"

His mouth dropped open, his eyes widened, and with a stunned look he quickly said, "Yes, very immoral, and I have been for some time."

I was so relieved to discover that his antagonism and persuasive argument stemmed from a determination to justify his sins that I'm afraid I almost squealed with delight. I told him strongly that I now knew his bold arguments came from a heart aching from a stricken conscience. I pled with him to forsake his sins and to go to his bishop and confess. He very humbly acknowledged that he would, and he did! Some months later, he married a non-member sweetheart, and what a thrill to learn that in less than two years, due to the completeness of his repentance, his wife became converted and they were married in the temple.

Members of the Church who are critical of the Lord's anointed are generally suffering from pride or from individual sin, both of which keep a person from enjoying the Spirit, without which one cannot build up the kingdom and obtain for themselves the promise of eternal life.

Knowing by Direct Light

As indicated in the chapter on being born again, one of the indications that we've actually experienced that most important event is our willingness to fully sustain the Lord's anointed. President Harold B. Lee confirmed this idea when he declared:

> That person is not fully converted until he sees the power of God resting upon the leaders of this Church and until it goes down into his heart like fire. Until the members of the Church have that conviction that these men of God are inspired and have been properly appointed by the hand of God, they are not truly converted. (Harold B. Lee,*Ensign*, July 1972, p. 203.)

In effect, our willingness to accept and sustain the Lord's anointed is in direct proportion to the influence and power of the Spirit in our lives. We simply cannot and will not see the mantle of divine authority resting on the Lord's anointed unless we are filled with the same spirit of prophecy that they have. Another way to put it is that it takes a prophet to know a prophet! Surely that is what Moses hoped and prayed for when he said, "Would God that all the Lord's people were prophets, and that the Lord would put his spirit upon them!" (Numbers 11:29.)

What I'm referring to is much more than receiving a witness that the leaders of the Church are prophets, but rather enjoying the consistent, regular companionship of the Holy Ghost that empowers one to accept, understand and do the bidding of the prophets. The Church has consistently urged the Saints to live on direct light, to know for themselves that they are being led by a prophet. Brigham pled with the Saints to catch the same vision the prophets have when he said the following:

> I am more afraid that this people have so much confidence in their leaders that they will not inquire for themselves of God whether they are led by Him. I am fearful they settle down in a state of blind self-security,

trusting their eternal destiny in the hands of their leaders
with a reckless confidence that in itself would thwart the
purposes of God in their salvation, and weaken that
influence they could give to their leaders, did they know
for themselves, by the revelations of Jesus, that they are
led in the right way. Let every man and woman know, by
the whispering of the Spirit of God to themselves,
whether their leaders are walking in the path the Lord
dictates, or not. (*JD* 9:150.)

A classic example of what Brigham Young was referring to is
found in the reaction of Lehi's sons to his revelations and
admonitions. All of them heard what was surely a powerful
testimony of what their father had seen and heard. In my
judgment, all four of Lehi's sons knew in their hearts that their
father's words were true. But of the four, Nephi was the only one
who really wanted to know more fully of that of which his father
had spoken—indeed, he wanted to see and hear and know without
question, so he went off by himself, and inquired of the Lord in
mighty prayer (1 Nephi 10:17). His heart was softened, and he
knew by direct experience that his father was inspired of the Lord.
Having caught the same vision enjoyed by his father, Nephi put
his hand to the plow and with power, constantly sustained his
father and fulfilled all the commandments of the Lord.

Thy Name is Written in Heaven

One of the most beautiful experiences I've read that shows the
blessing of sustaining *all* the words of the Lord's anointed is an
experience of Heber C. Kimball's. It was the spring of 1839. Joseph
was in jail; the persecution was terrible. On the 6th of April he
wrote:

My family having been gone about two months, during
which time I heard nothing from them; our brethren

being in prision; death and destruction following us everywhere we went; I felt sorrowful and lonely. The following words came to my mind, and the Spirit said unto me, "write," which I did by taking a piece of paper and writing on my knee as follows:. . . . "Verily I say unto my servant Heber, thou art my son, in whom I am well pleased; for thou art careful to hearken to my words, and not transgress my law, nor rebel against my servant Joseph Smith, *for thou hast a respect to the words of mine anointed, even from the least to the greatest of them; therefore thy name is written in heaven, no more to be blotted out forever.*"(Orson F. Whitney, *Life of Heber C. Kimball,* Salt Lake City: The Kimball Family, 1888, p. 253; emphasis added.)

May we sense deeply the tremendous importance of living prophets. May we come to know that our very salvation is dependent upon our honoring and sustaining the Lord's anointed—that if we will fully and completely accept the Lord's anointed, he, the Lord, will fully and completely accept us. Particularly may we come to realize that faith in Jesus Christ demands without exception faith in those he sends, and that a desire and hope to know Christ are inextricably tied to an acceptance of the Lord's anointed.

Chapter 9

To Know The Lord Is To Know Him As A Loving Father And To Know That We Can Acquire His Divine Love

My father was a very warm, loving man. Often as a child when I would hear his car drive up, I would run excitedly out of the house and leap off the stairs into his waiting arms. Invariably, he would hold me for a few moments, give me a big hug and a squeeze, and make some positive comments about me, so that by the time he set me down there was no question in my mind that my dad really loved me.

After my first quarter of college at Logan, Utah (which was the first time I had been away from home for any length of time), my reunion with my father was really something. When I drove into the farm yard, he came running out of the house and as we came together we didn't shake hands or even exchange greetings—

199

neither of us could speak! We simply threw our arms around one another, embraced, and kissed.

Throughout my life, the love my father and I have shared has been one of the greatest blessings I have known. Would we expect any less of a personal relationship with Christ? Would we imagine the Savior less warm and affectionate, less concerned and loving than an earthly father? Obviously not. I'm convinced that as members of the Church, we can arrive at a point where the Savior's love for us and our love for him will be the greatest source of joy in our life.

An experience that testifies most eloquently of the warmth and personal affection of both the Father and the Son is the following from Heber C. Kimball:

> During this time shortly after the dedication of the Kirtland Temple many great and marvelous visions were seen, one of which I will mention which Joseph the Prophet had concerning the Twelve...he saw the Twelve going forth, and they appeared to be in a far distant land. After some time they unexpectedly met together, apparently in great tribulation, their clothes all ragged, and their knees and feet sore. They formed into a circle, and all stood with their eyes fixed upon the ground. The Savior apppeared and stood in their midst and wept over them, and wanted to show Himself to them, but they did not discover Him. He (Joseph) saw until they had accomplished their work, and arrived at the gate of the celestial city; there Father Adam stood and opened the gate to them, and as they entered he embraced them one by one and kissed them. He then led them to the throne of God, and then the Savior embraced each one of them and kissed them, and crowned each one of them in the presence of God . . .the impression this vision left on Brother Joseph's mind was of so acute a nature, that he never could refrain from weeping while rehearsing it. (Whitney, *Life of Heber C. Kimball*, pp. 105-106.)

The beautiful love portrayed in this experience is charity and it is the love the Lord is anxious to bestow on us. It is important for us to understand what charity is, why we need it, and how we may obtain it.

What Charity Is

In 1 Corinthians Chapter 12, Paul the apostle elaborates on different gifts of the Spirit—special endowments available to those who have accepted the Christ as their Redeemer, who have been baptized of the water and of the Spirit. Paul emphasizes that each gift is important for the proper functioning of the church and the proper development of the individual members. However, after stressing the importance of these gifts, he concludes the chapter by saying, "And yet shew I unto you a more excellent way." Paul then delivers his great discourse on charity, declaring that even though one could prophesy, understand all mysteries and all knowledge, and have enough faith to move mountains, if he didn't have charity, he was nothing. He further testifies that even though an individual fed the poor and gave his body to be burned, if he didn't have charity, he was still nothing. After elaborating on the qualities and characteristics—longsuffering, kindness, lack of envy and so forth—of one who has charity, Paul concludes by saying, "And now abideth faith, hope, charity, these three; but the greatest of these is charity.

Paul teaches us that charity is a gift of the Spirit and that it is the greatest gift men and women can possess, but he does not tell us exactly what charity is; in fact, nowhere in those two chapters does he even mention the word love. It is Mormon who opens the door of our understanding and tells us simply and beautifully that *charity is the pure love of Christ* (Moroni 7:47). In other words, if we possess charity, we will have as a gift of the Spirit an endowment of love so great that we can love even as God and Christ love! What a marvelous contribution to our understanding—our spirits fairly soar to the heights to know that here on the earth we can receive an endowment from God that enables us to love Christ, ourselves, and others with the same love the Father and the Son have for everyone! In accordance with Paul's definition of charity as the greatest gift of the Spirit, Mormon stresses that charity, the "greatest of all," is "bestowed upon all who are true followers of his (God's) Son, Jesus Christ." In the context of the Book of Mormon, this great prophet is testifying that only through the ordinances and principles of the Gospel can men and women acquire this greatest gift of all.

Charity, then, is love, but it is a greater love than the love available outside the ordinances and principles of the restored gospel. The ability to love others and consequently to serve them is almost as universal as life itself and is, I believe, a quality all mankind enjoys through the light of Christ. Men and women do not have to embrace the gospel or, for that matter, believe in God to enjoy a remarkable love one for another. If the world is capable of such marvelous manifestations of kindness and service outside the gospel, think of the kindness and service possible with the greater blessing of charity. In fact, to compare the love available through the light of Christ to the great love, charity, would be like comparing the brightness of the moon to the brightness of the sun.

Even in the Church, we often fail to realize the difference between the love enjoyed by mankind in general and the greater endowment of charity. During the Savior's ministry, he was asked by a lawyer which was the greatest commandment. The Savior told him that the first and great commandment was to "love the Lord thy God with all thy heart, and with all thy soul, and with all thy mind. . .and the second is like unto it, Thou shalt love thy neighbour as thyself." However, just previous to the Savior's betrayal, He transcended the latter part of that first great commandment when he declared to his apostles, "A *new* commandment I give unto you, that ye love one another *as I have loved you.*" (John 13:24.) That was indeed a new commandment, an indication by the Savior of a much greater love than simply loving our neighbors as we love ourselves. How careful we need to be as Latter-day Saints to make sure we are enjoying the greater love—to make sure we are not content only with the love known by the world and consequently are not tasting of the love that comes as a gift of the spirit to faithful members of his church and is a gift that surpasseth all understanding.

Why Do We Need Charity?

The great work of God and his Christ is to bring to pass the immortality and eternal life of man (Moses 1:39). That work is accomplished through the atonement of Christ, which was prompted because "God so loved the world, that he gave his only begotten Son, that whosoever believeth in him should not perish, but have everlasting life." (John 3:16.)

An important reason all people need the pure love of Christ is that *out of that love, and that love only, comes enough power to keep the commandments of God.* "If ye love me, keep my commandments," the Lord said (John 14:15). As we grow in the Savior's godly endowment of love, we will increase in our ability to keep the commandments until "when he shall appear, we shall be like him." (Moroni 7:48.) In other words, it is charity that enables us to become sufficiently Christlike to "...inherit that place which thou hast prepared in the mansions of thy Father." (Ether 12:34).

A second fundamental reason we need charity is because when we are endowed with the Savior's pure love, we will have the desire, the determination, and the ability to assist in the redemption of God's children.

We can't be filled with the pure love of God without our sensing the infinite worth of everyone. We will find ourselves exclaiming, like Brigham, "The least, the most inferior person on earth is worth worlds." (JD 9:124.) We will sense the worth of everyone so deeply that we will find greater and greater opportunities to bless the lives of others. We will discover that the greatest need all people have is to know they are loved and loved deeply and that when they discover they are really loved, they will lay down their sins, turn away from transgression, and believe in themselves again. We will be willing to expend great energy and time in prayer, searching the scriptures, fasting, and sacrificing many ways so that we will have the power and ability to successfully entice people to come all the way to the Father through Christ.

After partaking of the tree of life, which is symbolic of enjoying a fulness of God's love through Christ, Lehi was so moved by what that experience meant in terms of receiving fully the blessings of the atonement that he immediately did all in his power to persuade his wife and his family to come and partake. You and I cannot taste of the Savior's love without finding it most natural to do all in our power to bring others to the same experience.

When Enos received a remission of his sins after praying all day and into the night, a great love came into his heart and he said, "I began to feel a desire for the welfare of my brethren, the Nephites: wherefore, I did pour out my whole soul unto God for them." (Enos 9.) After Enos received some assurances about future blessings for the Nephites, the intensity of his new-found love was so great that it transcended tradition and cleared the bounds of racial barriers, for he approached the Lord again with "many long strugglings for my brethren, the Lamanites" until he received the promise of the Lord that they indeed would be remembered and blessed by him.

The Lord was able to work a marvelous work through Enos by granting him charity. I believe all of us are almost startled when from time to time we feel so deeply the Lord's love for others. Such was the case with myself in the following encounter with a precious student of mine. This young lady was in one of my classes and I had noticed that she seemed unusually unhappy. One day after class, she came up to me and in a rather demanding tone indicated she had to talk to me. I told her when my office hours were and invited her to come.

A few days later, she came to my door and knocked. As I opened the door and greeted her, she responded with, "Brother Pace, I just came by to tell you what a rat I think you are! I can't stand what you teach!"

My initial reaction was defensive. However, I had learned from past experience that generally when a student comes on that negatively, they are, in effect, crying out for help. So in spite of my wounded ego, I forced a smile and said, "Come in and tell me more!"

At that time, large pictures of each of my children hung on the office wall, and as she entered she said, just a little belligerently, "Well, are these your children?"

I responded with an enthusiastic "Yes!"

She then asked, with a little less harshness in her voice, "Do you love your children?"

I answered, "Oh yes, I do."

Then, with a tender voice, she quietly enquired, "Do your children know you love them?"

I said, "Yes, yes, I think they do. I try to put my arms around them every day, hold them close and tell them how much I love them."

I'll never forget the look that came upon her face. She didn't say anything with her lips, yet she communicated as if with the voice of thunder. The message was "Brother Pace, do you know what it would mean to me if someone were to put their arms around me and tell me they loved me?"

The feelings of love that came into my heart were almost more than I could bear as I said, "I want you to know that I know the Lord loves you with an infinite love; and the reason I know that is because I feel, coming from him, such a great love for you! That experience commenced a friendship that over the years has been a choice experience for our whole family and has seemed to be a great strength to her.

Those who are endowed with charity will also find, as did Enos, that their love reaches out to those who would be considered their enemies. Probably one of the great examples I have read of an individual receiving an endowment of godly love enabling him to love his enemies is the following experience of George F. Richards:

> I dreamed that I and a group of my associates found ourselves in a courtyard where, around the outer edge of it, were German soldiers—the Fuehrer Adolph Hitler was there with his group, and they seemed to be sharpening their swords and cleaning their guns, and making preparations for a slaughter of some kind, or an execution. We knew not what, but, evidently we were the objects. But presently a circle was formed and this Fuehrer and his men were all within the circle, and my group and I were circled on the outside, and when we walked around and I got directly opposite him, I stepped inside the circle and walked across to where he was sitting and spoke to him, in a manner something like this, "I am your brother. You are my brother. In our heavenly home we lived together in love and peace. Why can we not so live here on the earth? And it seemed to me that I felt welling up in my soul, a love for that man, and I could feel he was having the same experience, and presently he arose, and we embraced each other and kissed each other, a kiss of affection. Then the scene changed so that our group was within the circle, and he and his group were on the outside, and when he came around to where I was standing, he stepped inside the circle and embraced me again with a kiss of affection.
>
> I think the Lord gave me that dream. Why should I dream of this man, one of the greatest enemies of mankind, and one of the wickedest, but that the Lord should teach me that I must love my enemies and I must love the wicked as well as the good?
>
> Now, who is there in this wide world that I could not love under those conditions, if I could continue to feel as I felt then? I have tried to maintain this feeling and,

thank the Lord, I have no enmity toward any person in this world. I can forgive all men, so far as I am concerned, and I am happy in doing so and in the love which I have for my fellowmen. (*CR* October 1946.)

The following story about a converted Indian by the name of Chief Blue illustrates dramatically what the love of Christ can do in blessing one with the ability to forgive:

One day my eleven-year-old son went hunting with six other Indians. They were hunting squirrels. A squirrel darted up a pine tree and my son climbed up the tree to scare him out on a limb. Finally, the squirrel ran out where he could be seen. My boy called to the hunters to hold their fire until he could get down out of the tree. One of these Indians in the hunting party had always been jealous of me and my position as chief. He and his son both shot deliberately at my boy. He was filled with buckshot from his knees to his head. One blast was aimed at his groin and the other hit him squarely in the face. The Indians carried my boy toward our home and found a cool spot along the trail under a pine tree. There they laid him down and ran for a doctor.

A friend came to me in Rock Hill where I had gone to buy goods and said, "Sam, run home at once, your boy has been shot." I thought it was one of my married sons. I ran all the way home and found that it was my little boy near death. The doctor was there. He had put the boy to sleep with morphine so he wouldn't be in so much pain. He said my boy could not live. He was right; the boy died in a few minutes.

The man and his son who had done the shooting were out in my front yard visiting with members of the crowd that had gathered. They did not appear to be upset at their deed. My heart filled with revenge and hatred . . . something seemed to whisper to me, "If you don't take down your gun and kill that man who murdered your son, Sam Blue, you are a coward."

Now I had been a Mormon ever since I was a young lad, and I knew it would not be right to take revenge. I decided to pray to the Lord about it. I left the house and walked to my secret place out in the timber where I always have gone to pray alone when I have a special problem, and there I prayed to the Lord to take revenge out of my heart. I soon felt better and I started back to the house. When I approached the house, I heard something inside of me whisper, "Sam Blue, if you don't kill that Indian who shot your boy, you are a coward!" I turned around and went back to my place of prayer and prayed again until I felt better. Then on my way back to the house at the same spot along the path I heard the voice say again, "Sam Blue, you are a coward." I turned again and went back to pray. This time I told the Lord he must help me or I would be a killer. I asked him to take revenge out of my heart and keep it out. I felt good when I got up from praying. I went back to the house the third time and when I reached the house, I went out and shook hands with the Indian who killed my boy—there was no hatred or desire for revenge in my heart. (*Speeches of the Year*, Marion G. Romney, February 1960.)

Almost every day I meet people who have been deeply wronged or profoundly hurt by others. I'm convinced that only by possessing the pure love of Christ as an endowment of the spirit can we obtain the ability to totally and completely forgive others and love them with a perfect love.

Charity reaches into every area of the life of a faithful Latter-day Saint. Those who enjoy this gift will rejoice in their knowledge of Christ, they will be pleased to bear testimony of him at all times and in all places (Mosiah 18:9). They will seek for the Spirit in all they do, that they might have the power to bring souls to the

Father through Christ. As part of their efforts, they will very spontaneously and naturally love everyone they come in contact with and perform acts of kindness to everyone in need.

This idea is expressed so beautifully in the parable given in the 25th chapter of Matthew. Previous to giving this parable, the Savior had spent his ministry emphasizing that no one would enter into the kingdom of heaven save they were baptized of the water and the Spirit and kept his commandments. In this chapter, he describes ever so effectively how his faithful members have conducted themselves in earth life in acts of kindness to the poor, the hungry, the naked, and others in need, and that in so doing, they have become fully acceptable to him!

The parable is portrayed in the pastoral setting of sheep and goats, the sheep representing the truly faithful in Christ, those who are acceptable to him, and the goats representing those who do not fully accept him or his gospel. I'd like to paraphrase that great drama.

When the righteous become aware that they are acceptable to the Lord, they seem almost surprised. One can almost hear one of the faithful say, "You mean I made it? My mortal probation is over and I'm acceptable to you? You mean I'm yours forever?"

And the Lord replies, "Yes, yes, your name is sealed in the Lamb's book of life forever!"

The faithful one, still somewhat incredulous, replies, "Oh, I so wanted to be faithful; however, I often felt so inadequate. How come I made it? I'm so grateful, but frankly, I'm overwhelmed. How is it that I am acceptable to you?"

The Lord replies, "Because *I* was hungry and you fed *me*. I was naked and *you* clothed *me*."

The faithful saint, simply not understanding, exclaims, "I don't ever remember doing that for you!"

And the Lord simply, but so profoundly, says "Inasmuch as ye have done it unto one of the least of these my brethren, ye have done it unto me." (Matthew 25:40.)

Nothing is so comprehensive, vast, and majestic as the theology of the Gospel of Christ. Yet after all the meetings have been held, the sermons given, the tithes and offerings paid, that theology must be translated into a transformed heart and soul, a human being so touched by the finger of the Lord's love that his whole ambition is to lift, bless, and comfort everyone he comes in contact with, that he might successfully entice people to come to the Father through the mercy, merits, and grace of Christ.

The Key to Obtaining Charity

Mormon, in his great discourse on charity, quite literally commands us to "pray unto the Father with all the energy of heart, that ye may be filled with this love." (Moroni 7:48.) In other words, the very key to the acquisition of charity is that we pray mightily for it!

To give you an illustration of the blessings that come by persisting in prayer for charity, I would like to share with you the following experience. However, I would like to emphasize that prior to this experience I had searched the scriptures and the writings of the brethren for an understanding of what charity is; I had tried to be very serious about magnifying my callings; and I had prayed with all of my heart for the endowment of charity.

I was teaching institute classes on campus at Stanford University while the Institute building was being constructed. This particular day of which I speak had been about as perfect as any day I could remember. Each class had gone well, the discussions were lively and the spirit was present.

In the evening I taught a class from 8 to 10 PM. After the class there was informal chatting and some counseling so that by the time I walked over to the house we were living in, which was on the edge of campus, it was quite late. As I approached the house I noticed all the lights were out and upon entering and checking the bedrooms I became aware that my wife and children were retired and sound asleep.

Because the day had gone so well, my spirit seemed unusually alive. The last thing I wanted to do was go to bed, so I went into the front room and sat on the edge of the couch. Immediately, I found myself mentally counting my blessings. I thought to myself, what a privilege it is to be alive, to have health and strength, to know who the Lord is, and to have tasted so deeply of his goodness; what an honor to have the priesthood and the gift of the Holy Ghost. There also came into my heart an almost overwhelming sense of gratitude for my precious wife and for our many children. As I continued to reflect on the Lord's graciousness to me, the gratitude I felt grew until it seemed every cell of my body was alive with the Spirit. Maybe the best way to put it is to say my cup was full and even running over.

After twenty minutes or so, I got up off the couch and quietly went into the bedroom where my wife was asleep. Without touching her or the bed, I knelt down close to her and in silent but mighty prayer, I told the Lord how grateful I was for her and how especially appreciative I was for her willingness to go, as it were, into the Valley of the Shadow of Death to bring so many of Heavenly Father's offspring along the frail path from his presence to mortality. I continued for some time to pray especially that the Lord would bless my wife with the Spirit, that her body would be renewed, and that she might have the health and strength she desperately needed to carry the heavy responsibilities that were hers.

I then knelt beside the sleeping form of my oldest daughter and expressed profound appreciation for her, remembering her concerns and anxieties. I did the same for each of my children. By the time I was through, it was quite late, and the feeling of gratitude had increased immeasurably.

I returned to the front room, and still feeling no desire whatsoever to retire, I thought I would conclude the day with verbal prayer. I prayed for an extended period of time, but finally starting to feel tired, I wondered if perhaps I should go to bed. But at that moment, a strong impression came to me that I should not retire, but rather that I should continue in prayer, which I did.

When my wife and I were married in the Salt Lake Temple, I really felt that I knew what love was all about. But over the years that love had continued to grow and develop to where I honestly wondered if it could be any greater. However, that night, as I persisted in prayer, there came an endowment of love that transcended anything I had tasted or felt previously in my life. Before that evening was over, I sensed, at least in a measure, what Nephi must have meant when he said, "He hath filled me with his love, even unto the consuming of my flesh." (2 Nephi 4:21.)

And what intensified feelings of love came first for the Lord, then for my wife and children, then my parents, then my brothers and sisters and their families; then it seemed to reach out for everyone and knew no bounds.

The endowment of charity is a literal, tangible bestowal of a dimension of love from the Savior that is beyond man's capability of describing. With the gift of charity, the majesty of the atonement, the power to keep the commandments, and the realization of the infinite worth of the souls of all of God's children will cause a joy that is almost more than a mortal body can bear!

Mighty prayer is the key to obtaining charity. We need to ask explicitly with all of the energy of our souls that we might receive that endowment. As time goes on, much of our effectiveness in prayer for others is because we have come to love them so dearly. I would counsel you to memorize Moroni 7:48 and not let a day go by without remembering Mormon's admonition and praying with all of your heart for that greatest of all endowments.

The greatest manifestation of the Father's love and of Christ's love is seen in their service in our behalf. It is natural, therefore, to anticipate that charity will come to us as we sacrifice much to build up the kingdom of God. If we lose ourselves in service in building up the kingdom, we will find ourselves wrapt up in the glory and love of the Savior. We all desire to return home to our Heavenly Father and to be warmly welcomed back into his presence. We will have that privilege if we obtain charity, the pure love of Christ, and are found still possessing that heavenly love when he comes in his glory. The one quality then that enables us to become like Christ and heirs of celestial glory is charity, the pure love of Christ. Charity is the capstone of a Christ-like character and by possessing it we will be prepared to return to and abide in the presence of our Heavenly Father. Brigham Young described in a beautiful way the intensity of that experience when he declared:

> "When you meet your Father in Heaven you will know him, and realize that you have lived with him, and rested in his bosom for ages gone passed, and he will hail you as his sons and daughters, and embrace you, and you will embrace him, and 'hallelujah, thank God I have come to Father again, I have got back home,' will resound through the heavens." (Manuscript History of the Church, p. 31.)

For I am persuaded, that neither death, nor life, nor angels, nor principalities nor powers, nor things present, nor things to come; Nor height, nor depth, nor any other creature, shall be able to separate us from the love of God, which is in Christ Jesus our Lord, (Romans 8:38-39.)

Chapter 10

To Know The Lord Is To Desire To See His Face While We Are Yet In The Flesh

If we had a friend we hadn't seen for years who sent us gifts that changed the whole course of our lives and made us supremely happy, would we not desire that we would have the opportunity of seeing him again that we might thank him personally for his great kindness to us?

We are in a similar situation with the Lord. He was our friend long before we came to the earth. He has bestowed upon us marvelous gifts that have changed our lives and made us supremely happy—gifts of such inestimable value that there is no way we could attach a price to them. How natural it is for us to want to meet him personally, to want to see him face to face, to thank him with all of our hearts for the blessings he has given us, to learn without question he is still our friend and that we have the promise of eternal life.

It is a righteous desire to want to see the Savior face to face and converse with him while we are yet in the flesh, to want to embrace him and learn for ourselves from his lips that he is pleased with our lives and that he is grateful for what we have done to try to build his kingdom. In fact, no faithful Latter-day Saint can be sanctified by the Spirit, grow in the knowledge of Christ, increase in the spirit of revelation, without there being born in his heart an intense desire to see the Savior. This desire will grow until it influences every thought, every action, and becomes the driving force to harmonize one's life totally with his mind and his will. We should also, however, be mindful that should we seek all our days to see the Lord while we are in the flesh and yet die before having that sacred experience, the seeking will be its own reward. Knowing we have sought with all of our hearts will give us a peace and an assurance that we are his and that we will yet see him face to face.

Obtaining the Desire to See the Face of the Lord

One day shortly after my mission, while irrigating sugar beets, I remember taking out of my pocket and reading the following experience related by a granddaughter of Lorenzo Snow:

> One evening when I was visiting Grandpa Snow in his room in the Salt Lake Temple I remained until the door-keepers had gone and the night watchman had not yet come in, so Grandpa said he would take me to the main, front entrance and let me out that way. He got his bunch of keys from his dresser.
>
> After we left his room and while we were still in the large corridor, leading into the Celestial room, I was walking several steps ahead of Grandpa when he stopped me, saying: 'Wait a moment, Allie. I want to tell you something. It was right here that the Lord Jesus

appeared to me at the time of the death of President Woodruff.'

Then Grandpa came a step nearer and held out his left hand and said: 'He stood right here, about three feet above the floor. It looked as though he stood on a plate of solid gold.'

Grandpa told me what a glorious personage the Savior is and described his hands, feet, countenance, and beautiful white robes, all of which were of such a glory of whiteness and brightness that he could hardly gaze upon Him.

Then Grandpa came another step nearer me and put his right hand on my head and said: 'Now granddaughter, I want you to remember that this is the testimony of your grandfather, that he told you with his own lips that he actually saw the Savior here in the temple and talked with him face to face.' (Lewis J. Harmer, *Revelation*, Salt Lake City: Bookcraft, 1957, pp. 119-120.)

How fully I felt the witness on that occasion that Lorenzo Snow literally saw the Savior in the Salt Lake Temple! The feelings that came into my heart were intense and I felt a great desire to someday see the Savior as did President Snow.

Another experience that has continued to give me great impetus in seeking to see Christ is the following experience of Melvin J. Ballard:

Away on the Fort Peck Reservation where I was doing missionary work with some of our Brethren laboring among the Indians, seeking the Lord for light to decide certain matters pertaining to our work there, and receiving a witness from him that we were doing things according to his will, I found myself one evening in the dreams of the night in that sacred building, the temple.

After a season of prayer and rejoicing I was informed that I should have the privilege of entering into one of these rooms, to meet a glorious personage, and, as I entered the door, I saw, seated on a raised platform, the most glorious being my eyes have ever beheld or that I ever conceived existed in all the eternal worlds. As I approached to be introduced, he spoke my name. If I shall live to be a million years old, I shall never forget that smile. He took me into his arms and kissed me, pressed me to his bosom, and blessed me, until the marrow of my bones seemed to melt! When he had finished, I fell at his feet and, as I bathed them with my tears and kisses, I saw the prints of the nails in the feet of the Redeemer of the world. The feeling that I had in the presence of him who hath all things in his hands, to have his love, his affection, and his blessings was such that if I ever can receive that of which I had but a foretaste, I would give all that I am, all that I ever hope to be, to feel what I then felt! (Bryant S. Hinckley, *Sermons and Missionary Services of Melvin J. Ballard*, Salt Lake City: Deseret Book, 1949, p. 156.)

The feelings that come into my heart every time I read that experience seem to form into questions: Who wouldn't desire to taste so fully of the love of Christ that it would seem the very marrow in his bones would melt? Who wouldn't give all they have or ever hope to have to obtain the privilege of dwelling in Christ's presence forever?

Perhaps because we rarely hear of instances where men and women are seeing Christ today, I was particularly encouraged and thrilled to read the following statement of President Harold B. Lee:

I know that this is the Lord's work, I know that Jesus Christ lives, and that he's closer to this Church and appears more often in holy places than any of us realize excepting sometimes to those to whom he makes

personal appearance. (Harold B. Lee, quoted in Living
Prophets for a Living Church, CES, p. 119)

A prophet who has had a great influence in my life is Joseph
Fielding Smith. The following quotation from that beloved prophet is choice because it is not only an invitation to see the Savior
from one who knew Christ so well, but a beautiful explanation of
what needs to be done to accomplish that goal:

> Now, what does the Lord expect of us when he says,
> 'Search diligently?' I think he wants us to seek His face,
> to call upon Him while He is near, to turn our hearts to
> Him. He wants us to seek righteousness, to seek an
> inheritance in His kingdom, to desire the association of
> clean, upright people both now and forever. (Deseret
> News Church Section, July 3, 1971, p. 11)

All of these testimonies have added to my desire to strive with
all of my heart to see the Lord. Without question, though, the
greatest fire that has entered my heart testifying to me that his
servants have seen him and that I, too, can see him, has come
when his anointed have testified that they know Jesus is the Christ
and while doing so the spirit of the Holy Ghost has confirmed to
my heart that they have seen Him and that I, too, can have the same
privilege. I marvel at the graciousness of the Lord in teaching me
that what they are saying goes far above and beyond the simple
words they are speaking. I can't express adequately my appreciation for those in leadership positions in the Church who have paid
the price to learn so fully who the Savior is and in bearing their
witness extend such a marvelous invitation for all of us to know the
Lord as well as they do.

It is important for us to realize that we can desire to see Christ
and seek with all of our hearts to do so without being a sign-
seeker. It is my understanding that we are not sign-seekers if we
have been pleased to believe in Christ and keep his commandments solely on the evidence of the workings of the Holy Ghost—

in other words, we seek to see him not so we will believe that he is, for we already have that witness; *but we seek to see him that in doing so, we might know we are acceptable to him and have become like him.*

Then Shall Ye Know that I Am

There are many beautiful invitations in the scriptures for men and women to seek to see Christ, but the most powerful invitation of all is found in D&C 93:1:

> Verily, thus saith the Lord: It shall come to pass that every soul who forsaketh his sins and cometh unto me, and calleth on my name and obeyeth my voice, and keepeth my commandments, shall see my face and know that I am.

Surely this scripture is one of the most comprehensive scriptures in all of Holy Writ. If we will come to know through a powerful witness of the Spirit that these words come from the Savior himself, and if we will keep them in our minds and hearts, they will transform our lives more than the words of any other single scripture!

Keeping in mind that I have attempted to have each chapter focus on different aspects of the central theme that we can develop a personal relationship with Christ, let's use this scripture to summarize the highlights of the doctrine of Christ that we have been studying in the foregoing chapters.

Every Soul

The Lord commences his invitation by saying, "Verily, thus saith the Lord: It shall come to pass that *every* soul. . ." The Lord is speaking to you and me, to everyone! Black and white, yellow and brown, men and women—everyone can qualify to see the Lord. It isn't a matter of rank or high position in the Church. The invitation transcends all boundaries. One of the greatest challenges we all have is to become convinced that the Lord has invited all of us to see him. Even those who have been faithful all their lives have a most difficult time accepting the idea that the Lord is serious when he says that everyone can see him. He wouldn't make the promise if it weren't possible to see him—he is speaking literally! The promise is true.

Who Forsaketh His Sins

Obtaining the ability to forsake our sins is a gift from the Savior. He pricks our hearts and causes us to sense that our lives are not right. He invites us to draw close to him. In our being willing to do so, he teaches us the stark seriousness of sin and promises us the power to forsake our sins if we will believe in him.

As we forsake our sins, we will be aware that the greatest and most common sins are sins of moral indiscretion. We will be tutored by the Spirit to know that if we will keep our hearts pure by forsaking sensual music, movies, television and literature, we have taken an invaluable step in mastering the body and becoming pure in heart.

Confession will play an important role in forsaking our sins, and if we seek the Lord's help, he will give us the courage to confess all of our sins to him and the courage to confess whatever sins we should confess to the bishop.

In following explicitly all the steps of repentance, we will realize that we cannot be forgiven unless our hearts are broken and our spirits are contrite. Repentance is a gift of the spirit and a necessary element in growing in the stature of Christ.

Who Cometh Unto Me

The Savior said, "Behold, I stand at the door and knock: if any man hear my voice, and open the door, I will come in to him, and will sup with him, and he with me." (Revelation 3:20.) The Lord is available to us—are we available to him? Are we really willing to open the door and invite him fully and totally into our lives? Are we keeping our eyes on Christ as we involve ourselves in the work of the Church, or are we so mechanical in what we do that our church activity is not transforming us or anyone else in the image of Christ? As we get our degrees, our professional training and learning, are we judging all things by and through the Savior?

We must keep our eyes riveted on the Savior if we ever expect the ordinances, principles, and programs to transform our lives. We need to realize that accomplishing what we need to accomplish will be predicted more *on our allowing the Savior to use us rather than our using the Savior.* He wants to use our minds, our hearts, and our bodies as tools in his hands to work a mighty work, and if we don't come fully to him, he cannot do so. To come unto Christ is to yield our hearts and whole souls to him that he might dwell in us and we in him, that we might become one and manifest his power, his purpose, and his love in all we do.

Who Calleth Upon My Name

King Benjamin added to our understanding of what it means to call upon the name of Christ by telling us "there shall be no other name given nor any other way nor means whereby salvation can come unto the children of men, only in and through the name of Christ, the Lord Omnipotent." (Mosiah 3:17.) Being so constantly battered with substitute names and substitute powers that promise relief from the evils of our day, it is refreshing to be reminded that the Savior and the Savior alone can offer us the way and the means by which we can be delivered fully from all sin, ignorance, and death.

Unfortunately, many people tend to give lip service to the name of Christ, but they actually seek for solutions to their personal problems, and development of their character from the reservoir of men's wisdom. Until we center our lives in the Savior and believe that by and through him we can become all we were created to become, we will enjoy nothing better than a terrestrial level of existence.

To "call upon my name" is to recognize the importance of mighty prayer, understanding that it is through Christ that our prayers are answered. It is to make contact with the Savior and to know he is blessing us and changing our lives. It is also to specifically and pointedly ask for the privilege of seeing him.

Long before we rend the veil and see the face of Christ, our prayers can be as "one man conversing with another." Long before we see our blessed Redeemer, it is possible through prayer to have felt of his spirit and power so strongly that we will wonder if we could know him much better by seeing him than we already know him. There isn't any one single thing that will do more to unlock the doors of heaven and allow the Savior to come totally into one's life than fervent, faithful prayer to the Father in the name of Christ.

Shall See My Face and Know That I Am

Those who have seen the Savior and have felt to share in writing their feelings give us a glimpse of the majesty of that experience. "Grandpa told me," Allie Young Pond said, "what a glorious personage the Savior is and described his hands, feet, countenance, and beautiful white robes, all of which were of such a glory of whiteness and brightness that he could hardly gaze upon Him." (Lewis J. Harmer, *Revelation*, Salt Lake City: Bookcraft, 1957, pp. 119-120.)

George F.Richards spoke of a dream in which he was in the presence of the Savior. Although the Savior didn't speak to him, Brother Richards felt a love that was beyond explanation, and he knew that love was revealed to him of the Lord. He afterwards said, "If only I can be with my Savior and have that same sense of love that I had in that dream, it will be the goal of my existence, the desire of my life." (Quoted by Ivan J. Barrett, "He Lives! For We Saw Him," *The Ensign*, August 1975, p. 21.)

Brother John Murdock, who boarded with the Prophet Joseph in Kirtland during the winter of 1832-33, recorded the following in his journal:

> In one of (the prayer meetings) the Prophet told us if we would humble ourselves before God, and exercise strong faith, we should see the face of the Lord, and about midday the visions of my mind were opened and the eyes of my understanding were enlightened, and I saw the form of a man, most lovely; the visage of His face was round and fair as the sun; His hair a bright silver grey, curled in a most majestic form; His eyes a keen penetrating blue; and the skin of His neck a most beautiful white. He was covered from the neck to the feet with a loose garment of pure white—whiter than any garment I had ever before seen. His countenance was most penetrating, and yet most lovely. And while I was endeavoring to comprehend the whole personage from head to feet it slipped from me, and the vision was closed up. But it left to my mind the impression of love, for months, that I never before felt to that degree. (Journal, p. 30, as found in the *Utah Genealogical and Historical Magazine*, Vol. 28, April 1937, p. 61.)

Although we can know the Savior in a remarkable way through the witness and nurturing power of the Holy Ghost, when we see him, we have a perfect knowledge of him. In that perfect knowledge comes a peace, comfort, strength, and intensity of love that categorizes the experience of seeing him as the single greatest experience mortal man can have.

I know the powers of heaven are real, that the Lord can and will make marvelous things known to us. I know the greatest lifting concept in the gospel is the belief that we can see Christ while we are yet in the flesh, and that we should strive with all our hearts to achieve that goal.

I know Jesus is the Christ, the Son of the living God. I know he appeared to the prophet Joseph Smith, and through that mighty prophet, restored his church and kingdom to the earth for the last time. I know that living prophets today have seen him and are receiving his mind and will for all who will harken. I know that the central reality of all life is Jesus Christ, and that the central purpose of all God's dealings with man is that each one of us might come to know the Savior fully. I know that the purpose of the Savior's life and atonement is to lift all mankind as high as they elect to be lifted, that families might be sealed in his perfect love and exist and abide through a never ending eternity.

May each one of us respond to the call to come to know the Lord and to seek to see his face, that we might each obtain the promise of eternal life.